PREACHER TALK

Herschel H. Hobbs

13

Broadman Press
Nashville, Tennessee

© Copyright 1979 • Broadman Press.

All rights reserved.

4227–05

ISBN: 0–8054–2705–8

All Scripture quotations are taken from the King James Version of the Bible.

Dewey Decimal Classification: 253.2

Subject heading: MINISTERS

Library of Congress Catalog Card Number: 78–73346

Printed in the United States of America

Dedicated to
all young preachers
with a prayer that your ministry
may be as happy as mine has been

Preface

I lay no claim to qualifications to write this little book other than the fact that I have spent fifty years trying to fill the demanding role of pastor of a local church. As you read it you will discover that no effort has been made to attain a depth of scholarship. I have deliberately strived for simplicity. Few references have been made to other books. The reason is that it is drawn from the well of personal experience.

Those who have had years of experience in the ministry will find what I have written somewhat commonplace. But I trust that even those will glean a helpful thought here and there. This book is written primarily with two groups in mind: those who are contemplating entering the pastoral ministry and those who are still young in such a ministry.

You will notice that I have written largely on the "I-You" basis. The "I" does not reflect egotism but personal experience. The "You" is used for direct application. Some years ago Dr. Andrew W. Blackwood, one of America's most renowned teachers of preaching, was asked what one suggestion he would make for the improvement of preaching. He said, "Say 'you,' not 'we.'" I have followed his suggestion in this volume.

If the reading of this book produces in young minds a better understanding of what is involved in being a pastor, helps to make some of the rough places smooth, and challenges the brave of heart to travel this road, then it will have accomplished its purpose. It is with a prayer to this end that it is sent forth.

HERSCHEL H. HOBBS

Pastor Emeritus
First Baptist Church
Oklahoma City, Oklahoma

3 John 2

Contents

1. What Is a Preacher? 9

2. Preach or Plow? 21

3. Sharp or Dull Axe? 34

4. Whither, Lord? 47

5. Pastor or Potentate? 59

6. Preparation or Plagiarism? 73

7. Prophet or Performer? 91

8. Mind Your Manners! 112

9. Say "We" 136

10. You Can Take Them with You . 153

    Epilogue 165

1

What Is a Preacher?

Some people think that there are four genders: male, female, neuter, and *preachers*. But every preacher knows that there are only three. Except in rare occasions they fall in the first category.

In an airport a stranger asked me, "Aren't you a preacher?" I replied, "Yes. But why do you ask?" He said, "Well, you just look like a preacher." As he walked away he left me wondering, *Just what does a preacher look like?* I was not wearing a clerical collar. I was not attired in a black suit, white shirt, and black tie. In fact, I was dressed the same as hundreds of other men in the airport. So the question persists, "What is a preacher?"

Preachers come in all shapes and sizes. Unfortunately, too many of us are out of shape and oversized. In recent years I have said that there are two kinds of preachers I do not like. One is a man my age who still has a head full of black hair. The other eats like a horse and is as skinny as a rail. No, really, I do not know of a single preacher I do not like and love. Admittedly it is easier to like/love some than others. In all honesty I am sure that some view me with the same mixed emotions. But all in all I feel that there is more genuine love among preachers than in any other group I know. And why should this not be the case, since we all love and serve the same Lord?But lest this treatment become "sticky" with sweetness, let us return to the question "What is a preacher?" And the answer in part is found in the question itself.

A Preacher Is a "What"

In dealing with the problem of misplaced loyalty to various preachers in the Corinthian church, Paul used himself and Apollos as examples. He asked, "Who then is Paul, and who is Apollos?" (1 Cor. 3:5). But the Greek text uses "what" rather than "who." He used the same Greek word for "any thing" (v. 7). The people were divided over them as personalities. But he said that they were but instruments used of God in his service. He did not deny that they were persons. Instead he emphasized their respective roles. "I have planted, Apollos watered; but God gave the increase. Now he that planteth and he that watereth are one: and every man shall receive his own reward according to his own labour. For we are labourers together with God" (vv. 6,8–9).

The Greek text reads, "For we are God's fellow labourers." This does not mean that we work with God with him on one side of the yoke and us on the other side. Paul said that he and Apollos were fellow laborers and that both belonged to God. To be sure, we work by God's power. But he does not work with us as equals. God's ministers are equals, but they belong to and work for God. Thus there is no true basis for rivalry between them. They have the same *owner* and work toward a common goal. Their responsibility is to please him, not men.

Since the ministry of both is necessary in God's plan, one should not be played over against the other. No preacher should ever knowingly and willingly be a part of church rivalry. Rather, he should faithfully point people to God, who is worthy of all praise and by whose power alone the preacher's work comes to fruition.

This same spirit was shown by John the Baptist. When asked as to his identity, he replied, "I am the [a] voice of one crying in the wilderness" (John 1:23). He did not say, "I am John the son of Zacharias the priest and of Elisabeth," but "I am a voice." Again, he did not deny his personhood. But he placed himself in the proper relationship with God as the voice through whom God spoke his message. Worthy of note is the fact that the last words of John recorded in the Fourth Gospel are, literally, "He [Christ] must go on increasing, but I must go on decreasing" (3:30).

The disciples of John the Baptist resented the fact that Jesus' ministry was surpassing that of their teacher. After all, did he not baptize Jesus and give him his start? To them he was gradually nudging John out of the picture. They had failed to grasp the purpose of God in the Baptist's ministry and the mission of Jesus. It takes a lot of grace for one preacher to rejoice over another preacher's success which exceeds his own. But John understood. He had done his work well. And he was content to step aside in favor of Jesus. He did not cease to preach until his arrest by Herod Antipas. But he was content to stand in the shadow as the sun of righteousness rose with healing in his wings.

Due to the prominence of his position and the attention shown him, every preacher knows the subtle temptation to think of himself as *someone special.* It is well for other people to think that. But woe betide the preacher who thinks it of himself!

Billy Graham told me that inordinate pride is the greatest temptation he has to resist. Wherever he goes people want to furnish him a large car and house him in a luxurious suite of rooms. For this reason he insists upon a small car and one private room with an adjoining room for his traveling assistant. Said he, "If I should give in to this temptation I do not believe I would live long. For the Bible says, 'I am the Lord: that is my name: and my glory will I not give to another' " (Isa. 42:8). Billy has had enough acclaim to make fools of preachers who are made of lesser stuff. I marvel that the more fame he achieves, the more humble he becomes. But, as shown by his own words, you can see that he has to work at it. Neither does he take pride in his humility. He goes right on being Billy as he points others to the Lord.

A preacher may give in to pride and continue to live physically. But it will mean death of his spiritual power and effectiveness. He should always remember that he is a "what" in God's hands for service. Truly great people are humble. It is the little person who feels that he must impress people who struts around like a peacock and demands recognition. You should not be concerned about this. If you deserve recognition, you will receive it. If you do not deserve it, you would not know what to do with it should you by some means receive it. It is far better to be great in God's sight than to let the plaudits of men dwarf your spirit.

A Preacher Is a Man

"There was a man sent from God, whose name was John" (John 1:6).

It is not my purpose to get into the argument about ordination of women. My purpose is to point out that a preacher is a human being. He is neither a semigod nor a superman. What spiritual power he has comes from God.

When Paul and Barnabas came to Lystra, Paul healed a lame man. The people thought that they were the gods Jupiter (Barnabas) and Mercurius or Hermes (Paul) come to visit them in bodily form. So they were preparing to sacrifice oxen to them. Seeing this, the apostles tore their clothes as a sign of great grief. They ran among the people, crying, "Sirs, why do ye these things? We also are men of like passions with you, and preach unto you that ye should turn from these vanities unto the living God" (Acts 14:15). In the Greek text "we" is emphatic. "Like passions" may well read "the same feelings." The only difference between them was that the Lystrans worshiped empty idols while the apostles worshiped the "living God." Their purpose in being there was to preach him to them, not to be placed on a pedestal of worship. If Paul declared himself as being only a man of like feelings with other men, certainly every preacher can say the same. Had Paul sought to benefit personally by this mistaken zeal, he would have been the toast of the town. Instead, outside the town he was stoned and left for dead. You should never seek to ride the wave of public acclaim. It is a fickle thing. But even if it does not turn on you and devour you, you will have betrayed the Lord's trust.

Believe it or not, preachers are people. They have the same strengths and weaknesses as do other people. They have the same bodily drives and experience the same physical temptations. In rare instances we hear or read where one yields to some gross sin. But, thank God, such cases are so seldom as to merit being front-page news.

However, apart from such, preachers become tired and confused. Their nerves can be rubbed raw. They do not have the pat answers to every situation any more than any other human being. At times they can be impatient with themselves and with other people. In such moments, like Moses, they may strike the rock instead of speaking to it as the Lord has said. Recently I saw this prayer on a pastor's desk. "Lord, give me patience— and do it right now."

Preachers try and fail. They have no magic wand by the waving of which they can get things done. In most instances they are dependent upon the voluntary cooperation of other people. Most business executives work with paid employees. When they say "Jump!" the employees simply ask, "How high?" It has been my observation through the years that when such executives are placed in charge of a church or a denominational program which relies upon voluntary cooperation, they need a preacher to prop them up.

Many years ago the minister of education and I worked out a program designed to enlist the men of the church in an intensive effort of visitation and ministry. When it was completed I showed it to the chairman of deacons, whose counsel I valued. After studying it he said, "Pastor, that is the most beautiful thing I ever saw laid out on paper. It has but one weakness—the human element. Will they do it?" To our sad disappointment, we learned that one weakness was fatal.

Yes, preachers try and fail. But seldom have I seen uncooperative laymen take the blame for failure. When the team is not winning, get a new *coach!* The trouble may be with the *team*, not with the coach. An ache in the head may be due to maladjusted bones in the feet. But the man at the top usually gets the blame.

When I was a boy in school, sometimes at recess we played a game called "The Man on Top Gets the Beating." Two boys would wrestle. But the object of the game was to stay on the bottom and not on the top. For the other boys stood around them, beating the one on top with boards. It is when church programs fail that both the pastor and his family need not the boards but the bolstering of those with whom he works.

Like other men, preachers have feet of clay. When under pressure if they fall from the pedestals upon which people have placed them, do not lose faith in them. Instead, remember that they are men of like feelings with other men. But it is for this very reason that they need to rely upon the grace and power of God. Certainly they should not continue to lie in the dust, but should get up and try again.

In a former pastorate a bank president was asked to serve as president of the Brotherhood. Having experienced a lack of cooperation in a project, he said to me, "Pastor, I do not see how you stand it!" I replied, "Well, I guess that when God calls a man into the ministry he gives him an extra supply of grace."

Paul found this to be true. We do not know what his "thorn in the flesh" was. We do know that three times he prayed for it to be removed. Instead, God said, "My grace is sufficient for thee: for my strength is made perfect in [thy] weakness" (2 Cor. 12:9).

So in the grace of God keep on keeping on. When you fail, try again! When you fall, get up and go again! God's grace is sufficient in such circumstances. Your very weakness may become a means for God to manifest his strength.

Recently, I was watching a baseball game on television. The batter hit a weak grounder to the pitcher. Instead of running toward first base with all his might, the batter took a few half-hearted steps and stopped. Yet so many things could have happened. The pitcher could have fallen down as he fielded the ball. He might have made a wild throw to first base. The first baseman could have dropped the ball. The manager fined the batter, not because he hit a weak ground ball but because after doing so he did not try.

One time you may hit the ball over the fence for a home run. Do not be overly proud when you do. You may hit a weak ball to the pitcher. But do not stop trying. You may reach first base safely if you try. But if you do not, at least you have the satisfaction of knowing that you did your best. Babe Ruth is famous for his home runs. But do you know that he also set an all-time strikeout record? When you swing for the fences, you are more likely to miss the ball.

The man who never made a mistake is working for someone who did. When you try, there is always the chance of failure. But there is an equal possibility of success. After all, you are only a man. But you are a man who serves a great God who never fails either us or in his eternal purpose. His grace is always sufficient to those who stand in the fierceness of the battle and/ or labor through the heat of the day.

A Man on a Mission

For legal purposes the Federal Social Security system classifies a preacher as "self-employed." But the Bible classifies him as a man on a mission for God. This was true of Moses (Ex. 3:1–10). It was also true of the prophets of the Old Testament (cf. Isa. 6:8–9; Jer. 1:4–10; Ezek. 2:3; Amos 7:14–15).

The same truth is expressed in the New Testament. John the Baptist was "sent from God" (John 1:6). The verb rendered "sent" means "sent forth." It is the word from which comes "apostle." John's mission was to be the Forerunner of Jesus as he prepared men's hearts to receive him (John 1:23; cf. Isa. 40:3–5). On resurrection Sunday night Jesus said to his followers, "As my Father hath sent me, even so send I you" (John 20:21). Paul was God's chosen vessel "to bear my name before the Gentiles, and kings, and the children of Israel" (Acts 9:15). It was their mission then, as it is every preacher's mission now, to prepare the way for

Jesus to be received into the hearts and lives of people everywhere.

This mission is expressed in two Greek words which are translated as *preach*. One means to evangelize or to bear the good news of God's redemptive work through Jesus Christ (Acts 11:20; 14:7). The other means to act as a herald. It was used of a king's herald who went throughout his kingdom declaring his message to the people. They were to hear and obey as though the king spoke to them in person. This word is used of John the Baptist "preaching in the wilderness of Judaea" (Matt. 3:1) and of Jesus preaching in Galilee (Matt. 4:17). Jesus used this word when he sent the twelve apostles on their mission. "And as ye go, preach, saying, The kingdom of heaven is at hand" (Matt. 10:7). Both of these words imply that those preaching were on a mission.

We speak of *missionaries*. This word is the Latin equivalent of the Greek word for one who is sent forth (apostle). Doctor Everett Gill, Sr. was a missionary in Europe for about thirty-five years. Shortly after his retirement he spoke in chapel at Southern Baptist Theological Seminary, where he was presented as a "foreign missionary." In response he said that he was just a missionary. The only *foreign* missionary the world ever knew was Jesus, who came from heaven to earth. Then Doctor Gill added that, like him, all of us were missionaries or sent ones. He was a missionary sent to Europe. We were missionaries sent to our student pastorates in Kentucky and surrounding states. We were all men on a mission.

As a man on such a mission, you are to concentrate on your task and not be deterred by lesser things. Due to economic necessities some preachers must earn a livelihood in the business world. But still their mission is to serve the Lord. Where such is not necessary every ounce of the preacher's energy and every moment of his time, other than time spent with his family, should be devoted to his mission. Even time spent sleeping or in necessary recreation should be for the purpose of strengthening his physical condition to be used in his mission.

As a Christian citizen the preacher is called upon to perform certain civic duties. But even here it can become a means to furthering his mission. However, caution should be exercised to prevent civic duties from becoming a substitute for his central calling. We must never permit the *good* to become an enemy of the *best.*

Billy Graham once told me that whenever and wherever he spoke to a public gathering, he always gave an invitation for people to trust in Jesus as their Savior. After all, he is a man on a mission, and that is his mission. When I am invited to speak at a civic club I begin by reminding the group that they invite people to speak in the area where they are most qualified. For me that is the gospel. So I preach a gospel sermon. If they do not want that they can get someone else. I am a man on a mission.

We should take a lesson from Nehemiah. As he and others were rebuilding the walls of Jerusalem, a group bent upon defeating his work sent for him to meet them for a conference. His reply is classic. "I am doing a great work, so that I cannot come down: why should the work cease, whilst I leave it, and come down to you?" (Neh. 6:3).

Many years ago I was guest at a civic dinner to honor a pastor of a large church who was leaving to assume another work. Civic leader after civic leader paid glowing tributes to him for his work in leading in so many worthy civic enterprises. But as I listened I could not help remembering that statistics showed that the previous year he had baptized only three people. He had forgotten his mission in favor of lesser undertakings.

Happily, this case is an exception to the rule. But one such is too many. This preacher was as busy as a bee. But in the scales of eternity his busyness left much to be desired. It was "much ado about nothing." Such should not happen to you and me!

It is said that if you should cut open the heart of a United States Marine you would find the American flag tattooed on the inside. Of course, this is but a figure of speech. But it tells us as preachers that inside our hearts should be the emblem of the kingdom of God. It is such a loyalty that will hold us to our task.

So loyal was Paul to his "heavenly vision" that as he faced the headman's block he could say in all honesty, "For I am now ready to be offered, and the time of my departure is at hand. I have fought a good fight, I have finished my course, I have kept the faith: Henceforth there is laid up for me a crown of righteousness, which the Lord, the righteous judge, shall give me at that day: and not to me only, but unto all them also that love his appearing" (2 Tim. 4:6–8). Certainly every preacher will love his appearing if he has been true to his mission.

A Man with a Message

The preacher's mission is meaningless without a message. Otherwise he will be only a gadabout. But the fact is that he is a man with a message. The Old Testament prophets did foretell the future. But the major burden of their ministry was to their own generations. To be sure, they spoke a message which was both timely and timeless. For truth is truth wherever and whenever it may be declared.

The prophets' messages were not their own but that of the Lord. Repeatedly they drove home their words with a "thus saith the Lord." Second Peter 1:20–21 states this truth: "No prophecy of the scripture is of any private interpretation." Actually this means that no prophet is a *self-starter*. The message came not "by the will of man: but holy men of God spake as they were moved [borne along] by the Holy Ghost [Spirit]."

The same principle applies in the New Testament. When Jesus sent his apostles on a preaching mission he told them what to do and say (Matt. 10:7–20). On resurrection Sunday night he interpreted his death and resurrection in terms of the Old Testament teachings. Then he told his followers that they were to bear witness of the same (Luke 24:44–49).

Paul was insistent that he did not receive his message from men but by a revelation given him by Jesus Christ (Gal. 1:12). To the Corinthians he wrote, "And I, brethren, when I came to you, came not with excellency of speech or of wisdom [like Greek philosophers], declaring unto you the testimony of God. For I determined not to know any thing among you, save Jesus Christ, and him crucified" (1 Cor. 2:1–2).

Some see in this statement that Paul failed in Athens as he attempted to preach philosophy on Mars' Hill (Acts 17:18–31) and that he had learned his lesson to stick with the theme of Christ crucified. However, an analysis of his sermon shows that he did preach the crucifixion (v. 31). The fact of the matter is that he adapted his message to the philosophy of his audience. And he did not fail (Acts 17:34). If on a given Sunday a pastor saw a Supreme Court justice saved, a woman of such prominence that her name merited mentioning, "and others with them"— that pastor could hardly wait for the "brag session" at the pastors' conference on Monday morning to tell about it. A strong church existed in Athens for a long time.

In 1 Corinthians 2:2 "to know" is a perfect infinitive. Long since Paul had come to know and continued to do so that "Jesus Christ, and him crucified" is the preacher's central message. He may deal with many themes. But ultimately he should come to Jesus Christ—crucified, risen, living, reigning, and coming again. "Christ is the Answer" is not simply a slogan. It is the central fact of life.

In 1959 Ramsey Pollard and I, with our wives, made a trip around the world visiting mission fields. In Japan and Korea we preached in revivals. Of Ramsey's preaching a Korean pastor said, "All he talks about is Jesus!" I told him that was the greatest compliment he will ever receive about his preaching.

One Sunday at the close of a service a woman said to Charles H. Spurgeon, "Mr. Spurgeon, I do not like your preaching. All you ever preach about is Jesus." To which he replied something like this, "Yes, Madam, that is true. No matter where I begin, I run across fields, jump ditches, and climb over hedgerows until I come alongside Jesus. Then I start to preach." I do not believe that you and I can improve on that.

Near the end of his public ministry Jesus went into an area

where John the Baptist had preached, but where he himself had never been. John 10:41–42 reads, "And many resorted unto him, and said, John did no miracle [sign]: but all things that John spake of this man were true. And many believed on him there."

"John did no miracle there." He did not heal the sick or raise the dead. But he faithfully proclaimed the message about Jesus. So much so that when the people saw him they recognized him and believed in him. This was written long after John had been beheaded. He did not live to see this fruit of his labor. But he had been faithful to his mission and message. And his ministry continued on after him. Like him, you and I will not live to see the total fruit of our labors. It will continue until the Lord comes again.

These verses may well serve as John's epitaph. No preacher can ask for any better.

2

Preach or Plow?

It is an old story, but it deserves retelling. A young man is said to have seen a sign in the sky: "GPC." He interpreted this to mean "Go Preach Christ." So he entered the ministry. But, as the old saying goes, he could not preach his way out of a paper sack. One of his members who was aware of his experience once remarked, "He thought that 'GPC' meant 'Go Preach Christ' when it probably meant 'Go Plow Corn.'"

Mrs. Hobbs' mother used to tell about two brothers she had known years ago. One was an intelligent, capable, and industrious farmer. The other was a somewhat odd, scatterbrained preacher. People said that God probably *called* the former brother, and the latter one *answered*.

However you may regard these two stories, I believe in a definite, divine call to the ministry. And I believe that if God calls someone to preach, he can preach. He may not be a Spurgeon, a Truett, or a Lee—but in his own way he can preach.

Furthermore, when the Bible speaks of the Lord's people being "peculiar," it does not mean that they are to be "oddballs." They are peculiar in that they are set apart as his servants to do a particular work for him. Of course, a separated people should be separated from the world and its evil system. They are to *stand out* rather than to *stand in*.

When Paul said, "I am made all things to all men, that I might by all means save some" (1 Cor. 9:22), he did not refer to entering into men's sins. He meant that he adapted himself, his message, and his method to fit the occasion of presenting Christ to people.

A skilled fisherman does not use only one lure. He selects the one designed to catch certain kinds of fish. Paul learned this lesson. And so should you.

Many Callings

In insisting upon a divine call to the pastoral/preaching ministry, one does not ignore the fact that God calls all his people to render service for him. Likewise, some are called to other definite phases of Christian ministry. I do not like the term "full-time Christian service" being applied to one particular group. All Christians are to render such a ministry. For instance, many years ago Charles Matthew wrote a book on soul winning. He called it *Every Christian's Job.* But we recognize that God does set apart certain people to fill a vocation in Christian service with no other means of economic support. And like the tribe of Levi, others are to provide for their livelihood. "The labourer is worthy of his hire" (Luke 10:7; cf. 1 Cor. 9:9; 1 Tim. 5:18).

Such "labourers" include *ministers* of education, music, business administration, recreation, and other similar areas of specified service. Happy is that pastor who has office clerical help who feel called to their work. Lucy Gibson, my secretary for almost twenty-five years, felt that she was *called,* not hired, to her work, as I did to mine. And she proved her faith by her works.

And do not forget those who *work with their hands!* Of course, there are "hirelings" who merely work for wages among the above categories as there are with some pastors. But I am thinking of the divine ideal.

God gave Moses instructions as to the making of the tabernacle and its furnishings and services (Ex. 25:1 to 30:38). Then he said, "See, I have called by name Bezaleel . . . and I have filled him with the spirit [Spirit] of God, in wisdom, and in understanding, and in knowledge, and in all manner of workmanship, To devise cunning works, to work in gold, and in silver, and in brass, And in cutting of stones, to set them, and in carving of timber; to work in all manner of workmanship" (Ex. 31:2–5). It was he whom God called to apply his skills and direction of others in building the tabernacle. Moses filled his role, and Bezaleel filled his.

Too often we tend to ignore those whose duty it is to see that we have a clean, warm or cool building with its appointments designed for effective study and worship. Their devotion to duty is as necessary for worship as songs and sermons. There are times when they are needed more than the pastor. If a water pipe bursts you do not call the pastor to come and pray over it; you call a plumber to repair it. As Nehemiah led in rebuilding the walls of Jerusalem, it was "every one unto his work" (Neh. 4:15).

Prophetic/Pastoral Call

I am certain that the Lord called me into the gospel ministry. When I was only five years old and people would ask me what I planned to be when I grew up, I never said fireman, train engineer, or cowboy. I said, "I am going to be a Methodist preacher like Brother Smith." At that time James Allen Smith was pastor of the Baptist church in Ashland, Alabama. To get to the Baptist church we went by the Methodist church. The names were mixed up in my mind. But I knew then I was going to be a preacher. Do not ask me to explain it, for I cannot do it. But somehow God had impressed it on my mind.

Incidentally, years later Dr. Smith and I were both pastors in Birmingham. One evening I spoke at a banquet in his church. In presenting me he told this story. I insisted that I had made as good a *Methodist* preacher as he had.

Yes, I know that I was called. It was many years later that I publicly surrendered to this call. But it was never out of my mind. Yet I cannot explain or describe it fully to anyone else, not even to another preacher. And I suspect that the same is true of other preachers.

One might detail circumstances. But such a dealing with us on God's part is so personal and spiritual that it is practically impossible to put it into words. However, it will prove helpful to study some of the most distinctive *calls* found in the Bible. We will deal with them under two categories: the *reluctant* and the *readily responsive.*

Strangely, one of the most reluctant was Moses. While he was destined to lead the children of Israel from Egyptian bondage, his call came in the desert near Mount Sinai when he was about eighty years of age. His life is usually divided into three periods of forty years each: in the royal court of Egypt, in the desert in Midian, and his work in delivering the Israelite slaves and molding them into a covenant nation under God. But our present concern is only with his call. For eighty years God had been preparing him for the work he was to do. But it is impossible to read the story of Moses' birth and subsequent events and fail to see that he was a child of destiny.

It was on "the backside of the desert" that God appeared to Moses in the burning bush, a bush which burned but was not consumed (Ex. 3:1–2). He was told to remove his shoes because he was on holy ground. Surely every person stands on sacred soil when God lays his hand upon him to call him into special service. Upon hearing God's purpose for him, Moses offered five excuses why he could not do it.

1. "Who am I, that I should go unto Pharaoh?" (v. 11). After all, he had a price on his head in Egypt. Besides, he was no crusader but a simple shepherd. He could not challenge the mighty ruler. God's reply was the promise of his presence.

2. Should he go, in whose name should he say he came? (v. 13). The Lord told him to say, "I AM hath sent me unto you." "I AM THAT I AM" (v. 14) actually reads, "He will be that he will be." It is a third person singular future form of the Hebrew verb "to be." From this comes the word *Yahweh* or Jehovah, God's redeeming name. So to Moses God revealed that he is about to be the redeeming one. Of interest is the fact that "Joshua" *(Yeshua)* is derived from this name. It means "Jehovah is salvation." "Jesus" is the Greek equivalent of this Hebrew word. Thus "Jesus" means "Jehovah is salvation" (Matt. 1:21). At the burning

bush Jehovah begins to reveal himself as the Redeemer or Savior, a revelation which finds its complete form in Jesus Christ.

3. Moses countered that the Israelites would not believe him (4:1). Then God gave him signs by which to prove that he had sent him (vv. 2–9).

4. With this Moses pleaded that he was not an eloquent speaker (v. 10). Some see this to mean that he had a speech impediment. But it more likely means that he was not a man good with words. His lonely desert life could have made him like this. But God reminded him that since he had made Moses' mouth, he could also enable him to use it (vv. 11–12).

5. Finally Moses revealed his real objection. He did not want to go (v. 13). Just send someone else. He was content to live and die as an anonymous shepherd. Shepherd sheep? Yes. But not people. Had God left him alone, his name would long ago have been covered by the desert sands, rather than being one of the greatest names of the ages.

God's patience was at an end (v. 14). He still did not let Moses off the hook. Rather, he promised that Aaron, Moses' older brother, would be assigned to help him (vv. 14–17). At this point Moses had run out of excuses. So he acquiesced.

Notice that God did not promise Moses that the task would be easy (3:19). When Jesus sent his disciples on a preaching mission, he said, "Behold, I send you forth as sheep in the midst of wolves" (Matt. 10:16; cf. Luke 10:3). On the night before his death he told the eleven apostles that as the world hated him, so it would hate them (John 15:18–21). But as Jehovah did to Moses, so Jesus did to his apostles. He promised his presence and victory. "In the world ye shall have tribulation [be in a tight place with seemingly no way out]: but be of good cheer [courage]; I have overcome [fully conquered] the world" (John 16:33).

To a lesser degree, Jeremiah was reluctant to answer God's call. This was true even though the Lord told him that before he was conceived in his mother's womb, "I ordained thee a prophet unto the nations" (Jer. 1:5). Jeremiah was overwhelmed by the thought. "Ah, Lord God! behold, I cannot speak: for I am a child" (v. 6). The Hebrew word for "child" could mean anyone under twenty years of age. We may assume that he was a young man in his late teen years. However, this was the only objection he offered. Again the Lord promised to speak through him.

There must have been a swimming in Jeremiah's head as he heard of the task assigned to him. He was to be over nations and kingdoms, not to rule them but to preach to them. Using the double figure of plants and buildings, God gave him his mission—first, negatively, and, then, positively. He was to root out plants of evil and to pull down (throw down) structures of evil (v. 10). "To destroy" means to leave to perish, suggesting the pulled-up plants. He was to throw down (break in pieces) the unwanted buildings. Then, having done these things, he was "to build" righteous structures and "to plant" that which would yield a harvest according to God's will.

Quite naturally, such a ministry would not make him popular with his contemporaries, as, indeed, he was not. At one point he was even regarded as a traitor to his nation. But time has shown that he was the most loyal subject in Judah.

God does not call you to win popularity contests. If you denounce sin, you can be certain to experience the wrath of an evil age which is in revolt against God. You will find that preaching truth is a thankless task in such a world. But in being faithful to your call you will please God, lead many to be saved, and deliver your own soul with respect to those who reject your message.

With this apparently Jeremiah offered no further objections. He was to get on with the work. He would meet strong opposition, as indeed he did; but in God's presence and power he would be both safe and victorious (vv. 17–19).

As we analyze these two men, we find that they had certain things in common. Both were born for a mission. Both were amazed that God would call them to so stupendous a task. As each measured his human capacity, neither felt that he was equal to the task. Who would listen to a shepherd from Midian or a young man under twenty years of age? Pharaoh claimed to be a god. Judah worshiped false gods. In neither case did the men think they would be successful as they spoke in Jehovah's name. Moses was not eloquent and Jeremiah would sound like a presumptuous child. But in both cases God promised them words to speak. Furthermore, he would be with them. If they got into hot water he would be in it with them.

But it all boiled down to the fact that neither wanted to undertake so gigantic a task (Ex. 4:13; Jer. 1:6). Yet in the end each accepted the role of God's servant. Moses would face seemingly insurmountable situations; his patience with people would be tried even to the breaking point. Suffice to say that Jeremiah was to become "the weeping prophet." But in so doing both Moses and Jeremiah walked into the pages of history.

I have heard many preachers tell of the struggle they had with God before surrendering to his call. Yet, with rare exceptions, I have never known one who seriously applied himself to the work but that he was happy in it. And I have never known one who, being called, refused it and was ever happy or truly successful in any other line of endeavor.

In Jesus' words to his apostles recorded in Matthew 16:25–26 he repeatedly used the word *psuche*. It may be translated as soul, as the principle of life, or as the real meaning of life. We do not do violence to his words if we use the second and third senses. "For whosoever may will to save his life [as he designs it], shall lose it [the real meaning of life]: and whosoever may lose his life [as he designs it] for my sake, shall find it. For what is a man profited, if he may gain the whole world, but may lose the real meaning of his life? or what shall a man give in exchange for the real meaning of his life?" (author's paraphrase).

Over against those who were reluctant to accept God's call, there were many who gave a ready response to it. When God called Noah to build the ark in a desert land, he began immediately to do so, probably amid the jeers of his contemporaries (Gen.

6:14,22; Heb. 11:7). At the Lord's command Abraham left home and family to go on an uncharted course into an unnamed land to which he was divinely led (Gen. 12:1; Heb. 11:8–10). Under the guidance of Eli the boy Samuel said, "Speak, Lord, for thy servant heareth" (1 Sam. 3:9). When in his temple vision Isaiah heard Jehovah ask, "Whom shall I send, and who will go for us?" he replied, "Here am I; send me" (Isa. 6:8). Not one murmur of protest is heard from Ezekiel when the Lord sent him on his mission (Ezek. 1—7). There is no evidence of hesitancy in Amos' heart when God sent him from his rural quietness to prophesy amid the gathering storm in Israel (Amos 7:14–15). Hosea did not question Jehovah when he led him through heartbreak that he might understand the Lord's love for his adulterous people (Hos. 1:2 to 3:5).

John the Baptist was born for a mission which as a man he readily accepted and performed (Luke 1:5–25,37–80; 3:1–17; John 1:6,15,19–37; 23–30). Without a moment of hesitation Peter, Andrew, James, and John left their nets to follow Jesus (Mark 1:16–20). Likewise Matthew (Levi) left his customs table to serve the Lord's table (Matt. 9:9). Saul of Tarsus was miraculously saved on the Damascus road (Acts 9). His first question thereafter was "What shall I do, Lord?" (Acts 22:10). And to the end of his life he "was not disobedient unto the heavenly vision" (Acts 26:19).

However, the point of all these examples is that once committed, whether hesitantly or readily, these servants of the Lord were faithful to their calling. None of them was to be "carried to the skies, On flowry beds of ease." As the song says, they "fought to win the prize, And sailed thro' bloody seas." But always they were conscious of the Lord's presence and power. He does not call us to a mission and then leave us to flounder through it alone. Always when the going is roughest he is there with words of encouragement and grace to enable us to carry on (Acts 18:9–10; 27:23–24; 2 Cor. 12:7–10). In the poet's words, he stands "within the shadows, keeping watch above his own."

In the Great Commission (Matt. 28:1–20) Jesus said, "And,

lo, I am with you alway, even unto the end of the world" or "age." "Alway" translates a phrase "all the days" or, more specifically, "every single one of the days." Good days and bad days; days of joy and days of sorrow; days of victory and days of defeat— all the days. This is a blessed promise indeed to you as you submit to God's call.

Does God Call Men Today?

The Bible says quite clearly that God called men during that period of holy history recorded in the Bible. If he did so then, why not now? Malachi 3:6 says, "For I am the Lord, I change not." And Jesus Christ is the same yesterday, and today and forever (Heb. 13:8). Even so, a secularized age tends to downgrade the sacred. Thus some, even some preachers, question the idea of a divinely called ministry. Admittedly there may be some in the ministry who were not called. But this is not necessarily the norm.

How apart from a divine call can you explain men like John Wesley and George Whitfield? Refused the right to preach in the pulpits of the established church in England, they preached in fields and factories. Historians credit them with saving England from a holocaust similar to the French Revolution. Dwight L. Moody, a shoe salesman with a meager education, is said to have rocked two continents, Europe and North America, toward God. I recall reading of an incident in his life. Following a sermon in which he had butchered the King's English a woman said to him, "Mr. Moody, I do not like your preaching! You use bad grammar!" He responded, "Well, lady, you use grammar good enough. What are you doing with it for God?"

What about Charles H. Spurgeon, one of the greatest of pulpiteers, whose preaching is said to have saved England from the Deism which flourished on the continent of Europe? Or Billy Sunday, who was transformed from a wild-living professional baseball player into one of the most effective evangelists of all time? Or Billy Graham, who has preached to more people than any man who ever lived? As I study him and his phenomenal ministry, I can explain it only by seeing the hand of God upon him, as indeed may be said of the others mentioned above.

But what about less noted preachers today? If God calls some, does he not also call others? Why he calls certain ones and not others is beside the point. The question is whether he calls those who serve in the ministry. Certainly men do not enter the ministry for the purpose of prestige. Who can know at the outset that he will achieve such? While some may rise to fame, thousands are like the flower which gave out its fragrance in the desert air. Surely it is not for the purpose of finding an easy job. There is no calling which makes greater demands upon one's physical, nervous, and spiritual energy. A preacher is on the job twenty-four hours a day—if not actually working he is *on call*. In more than forty-five years as a pastor I do not recall a single night when I put my car in the garage, knowing that I would not have to take it out again before daybreak.

A classroom for ladies had been redecorated. On the Sunday that they reentered it I went by to pay my greetings. The class president said, "We appreciate your coming by. We know that this is your *busy* day." I did not correct her, but smiled as I recalled that it was my easiest day in the week.

Most certainly one does not enter the ministry for financial gain. I do not know of any pastor but who, if he applied the same amount of native ability, energy, time, and training to some other field, could double or treble his income received as a pastor. And this goes for any other person who follows a religious vocation.

Why, then, does one enter the gospel ministry? Because he can say with Jeremiah, "But his word was in mine heart as a burning fire shut up in my bones, and I was weary with forebearing, and I could not stay" (Jer. 20:9). And he can say with Paul, "For necessity is laid upon me; yea, woe is unto me, if I preach not the gospel!" (1 Cor. 9:16).

Yes, the true preacher is confident that God has laid his hand upon him. If that be not true in your case, then you would be wise to spend your life in some other capacity. For you will soon learn that the ministry is no bed of roses. There is no field of endeavor which is more demanding. But it you are convinced that God has called you, you should be willing to spend and be spent. When the way is the hardest, you can find rest in the assurance that you are where the Lord placed you. Furthermore, you can claim the Lord's promise, "Lo, I am with you alway, even unto the end of the world [age]" (Matt. 28:20).

Determining God's Will

Every pastor is asked many times by his members, "How can I determine God's will for my life?" If this question is vital to other Christians, it is doubly the case with the potential minister. How can you determine if you are called of God to be a minister?

Of course, some know it instinctively. Even so, there comes that moment in your life when you must face up to the matter. You must say yes or no to God's call.

As for myself, I have noted already that I cannot recall any time in my life when I did not feel that the ministry was my calling. But there comes that moment when I had to say yes to God. I was about seventeen years old when I went forward one Sunday night to make a public surrender to the call to preach. It was in the Ensley Baptist Church, Birmingham, of which Dr. David M. Gardner, later editor of the *Baptist Standard* of Texas, was the pastor. In the years following I got away from this commitment. In the meantime Mrs. Hobbs and I were married. We were then members of the Brighton Baptist Church, near Bessemer, Alabama. Seeking satisfaction in my then present state, I accepted almost every job the church had to offer: deacon, Sunday School superintendent, choir leader—you name it.

In all honesty I must admit that I did not know one note from another. I had never heard of one, two, or three time in directing music. I simply rolled up a paperback *Modern Hymnal* like a club and beat time in my hand. My only qualification for the position of choir director and song leader was that I had more brass than anyone else. But regardless of what I did, no peace of mind came. Finally one night in a revival I made another public commitment from which I did not turn back. Not one moment since then have I regretted it.

But what about those who have no such innate sense of call? Yet the conviction of a call comes. Let me suggest a very simple approach to this. Ask yourself a series of questions: Does something need to be done? Do you feel that you have the qualities designed to meet it? Do you sense that God wants you to do it? Are you willing to let his will be done?

The final decision should be made carefully and prayerfully. Let God speak to you through his written Word as you read the Bible—especially those passages about the men cited earlier in this chapter who were called of God. Counsel with your pastor, Sunday School teacher, parents, and/or other friends whose spiritual advice you trust. Let your will be sensitive to the guidance of the Holy Spirit as he speaks to your heart.

Satan will put many obstacles in your path. He will tempt you with the allure and glamour of the world. He will offer many substitutes. Thus you would do well to read how he tempted Jesus in an effort to draw him away from God's will (Matt. 4; Luke 4). Let me remind you that the devil tempted Jesus in his humanity. And Jesus resisted in the same. Not once did he use his divine power. He resisted through meditation, prayer, the Bible, the Holy Spirit, and total submission to the Father's will. Each of these resources is available to you! And once having placed himself in the path of God's will, he never looked back.

The final decision must be yours alone. You must retreat into the innermost secret chamber of your soul. And there alone with God—convinced that it is his will—blend your will with his will. And never look back!

"Thy will be done." As a Christian these are the most important four words you will ever utter insofar as your own life is concerned. Thereafter, your words should ever be "What shall I do, Lord?"

And if asked in faith and sincerity, they will never lack for an answer.

Amazed at Being Called

Paul could never understand why the Lord called him into the ministry (1 Tim. 1:11–16). He said that he was the "chief" (first) of sinners (v. 15) and "less than the least of all saints" (Eph. 3:8). This greatest of all preachers felt that if someone should make a list of all sinners, his name should head the list. And should you list all the saints (Christians), at the bottom of the list you should drop down several spaces and there write his name (cf. 1 Cor. 15:9). The fact is that the nearer to the Lord you live, the greater is your consciousness of your sin. Likewise, you are aware of how undeserving you are. Still he could say that "by the grace of God I am what I am" (1 Cor. 15:10). It was precisely for this reason that he "laboured more abundantly than they all" (v. 10). But he hastened to add that God's grace had labored in or with him (v. 10).

Paul's attitude should characterize every minister of the gospel. We are but "earthen vessels"—so brittle—into which God has deposited his treasure of the good news of redemption through Christ (2 Cor. 4:7). Any preacher who feels that he *deserves* to be in the ministry does not. One of the subtlest of temptations confronting us is pride. This is especially true of the younger ones. It is the highest of all callings. But for that very reason we should be humbled by that fact. We are all what we are by God's grace. He does not honor us by making us such. Rather we should honor the calling by living honorably in it. Only thus may we expect to hear the "well done" of him whose we are and whom we serve.

3

Sharp or Dull Axe?

You can cut down a tree with a dull axe. But you can do it more rapidly and more neatly if the axe is sharp. God can use an untrained preacher. But one who is trained for his work becomes a more effective and efficient tool in his hands.

Recently I read about a small chain of food places called "Grandma's Fried Chicken." Its slogan was "If the Colonel Had Grandma's Recipe He Would Be a General." Somewhere in that slogan is a lesson for preachers.

At best preachers are imperfect people, but they should endeavor to present God with the best possible working tools. W. O. Carver once said, "God has no perfect individuals or institutions through which to work. He has to get along with us just the way we are the best he can." However, this is no excuse for a lack of preparation for the task to which the preacher has been called.

Necessity for Training

Regardless of what field of endeavor a person may enter, a period of training is necessary. During World War II I was a pastor in Alexandria, Louisiana. It was the most concentrated troop training area in the nation. Five army camps and several air bases were within a few miles of each other. As great as was the national crisis and the need for troops, many weeks lay between the time of induction into the military service and one's readiness for the battle area. The soldier's body must be developed to enable him to have strength and endurance. He must learn discipline, military science and tactics, and skill in the use of his weapons. Otherwise he would be a hindrance, even a menace to his comrades in arms.

The same principle applies in civilian pursuits. In industry a person must serve as a boilermaker's or a plumber's helper before he can become one himself. In any similar field a person must learn skills and how to use the tools of his trade. Whether one is to be a doctor, lawyer, scientist, accountant, or business administrator, he must give himself to years of rigorous training or education before he is ready to become active in his vocation.

Fans watch an athletic team play with precision. This is no spur-of-the-moment thing. It is possible because, far removed from the spectators' eyes, the team has gone through its plays over and over again. I once knew a football player of exceptional ability. On Saturdays he gloried in the cheers of the fans over his long runs. But he refused to go through the grime and sweat of practice during the week. Thus he became a problem to the coaches and team. Eventually he was dropped from the team. When he entered professional football, the same attitude took him from team to team. Finally, no team wanted him. So he dropped out of football to be swallowed up in oblivion. If he was so good without practice, how much better he would have been with it!

Who would want a young man fresh out of high school to perform a delicate operation on him? defend him in a lawsuit? fill out his income tax? manage a large corporation? The answer in each case is quite evident.

If such training is necessary in mundane things, it is far more a necessity in spiritual matters. Is not the spirit more important than the body? Are not spiritual matters more vital than legal or economic values? Since the answer to these questions is obviously in the affirmative, it automatically follows that one who proposes to follow God's call in heavenly matters should place a priority upon education and training for his task.

Someone asked a general what the most important thing is in

winning a military victory. He replied, "Making a good ready!" Another general said that battles are won the night before they are fought. These ideas say something to preachers.

Call to Prepare

It is a fitting adage that a call to *preach* is a call to *prepare*. Every young preacher knows the subtle temptation of seeing the world going to hell and feeling that he must immediately get into the thick of the battle in an effort to stop it. But the world has been on that course since Adam and Eve sinned in the Garden of Eden. It will continue in this way until Jesus returns.

I am not discounting the value of even one soul you may snatch from the jaws of eternal death. But by taking the longer look you may rescue even more souls from such a fate if you spend the necessary years to sharpen your *axe*.

In the hidden ages of the past, God knew what you now know about the world's trend. His redemptive purpose was in his heart before he made the first man. The Bible reveals how this purpose unfolded as the Father prepared for the sending of his Son to provide redemption. "But when the fulness of the time was come, God sent forth his Son, made of a woman, made under the law, To redeem them that were under the law" (Gal. 4:4–5). Whatever the meaning of "the fulness of the time"—it was a time right in God's merciful and gracious wisdom.

God has a purpose—to redeem man effectively. And he moves by a plan designed to that end. He also has a purpose for you in that plan. His purpose for you is that at the outset you "make a good ready" so that you will be most effective in that plan. And this calls for preparation to the degree of your opportunity. In his redemptive will God shows *purpose, plan,* and *preparation.* On your part you should do likewise in your own sphere.

Opportunities for Preparation

In his final letter written to his younger co-laborer, Paul told Timothy to "Study to shew thyself approved unto God, a workman that needeth not to be ashamed, rightly dividing the word of truth" (2 Tim. 2:15). Actually the word for "study" means "give diligence." "To shew" means to stand alongside or to present. The idea here is that of presenting yourself to God as a prepared workman. Several suggested meanings are given for the word rendered "rightly dividing." One is to plow a straight furrow. Another is that of a stonemason cutting the stones straight. These may well apply to you as a preacher. But since Paul was a tentmaker and knew how to cut straight the rough camel's hair cloth, "cutting straight"—leaving no ragged edges—seems to be the best sense here. Thus it fits the dual idea of a sharp tool and a skilled hand. For our purpose we may see you who have responded to God's call both to preach and to prepare presenting yourself to God as a workman with a sharp tool and a skilled hand, ready to be used in such a fashion as to be tested and proved genuine in God's service.

For the moment let us assume that you either have finished or plan to finish high school. One year before finishing high school I was offered a good job in a promising field, and was tempted to accept it. My mother urged me to finish high school; thus, should I ever want to attend college, I would be ready. I followed her advice, for which I will always be grateful. Even though almost four years elapsed between high school and college, when I fully surrendered to the call to the ministry I was ready to pursue further training.

At the time of this commitment Mrs. Hobbs and I were living with her parents. Her mother was pure gold, and she never wasted words. When I announced my decision, she said, "Well, you and Sis (Mrs. Hobbs' family name) will just get ready to go to Howard College (Samford University)." I said, "I can't go to college! I have a wife to support!" She replied, "Well, I don't care. If you are going to preach you must go to college. We don't want a jackleg preacher in the family!" Poor thing! In spite of it she wound up with one. But she did her best.

Now I am not saying that every preacher who does not go to

college is a "jackleg." I am simply reporting her conviction as
to the need for training in the ministry. We will return to this
matter later in the chapter. But I am saying that you should
have such a high regard for your calling as to avail yourself of
every available opportunity for education in preparation for your
work. Failure to do so reflects a wrong attitude toward the ministry, an attitude which will affect your work from that time on.
Opportunity will vary from case to case. But you are responsible
for utilizing fully the opportunity you have.

In due time Frances and I did enter Howard College. By that
time I was pastor of a small church in Birmingham. For six months
we had served the Vinesville Baptist Church, Birmingham, our
first pastorate. It was largely a Sunday and Wednesday night
responsibility. Since the salary was insufficient for a livelihood,
both of us had jobs in the business world. However, our goal
was to enter college. We had figured that we needed seventy-
five dollars per month on which to live (depression times). One
day I received a phone call from Fred Schatz, later a professor
at Carson-Newman College and professor and dean of Belmont
College, who was chairman of the pulpit committee of the Berney
Points Baptist Church, Birmingham. He invited me to preach
for them in view of a call, stating that they paid seventy-five
dollars per month! From that moment on we felt it was an answer
to prayer. We were called there, and remained until we graduated
from college.

In February 1930 we entered Howard College, later receiving
our degrees in August 1932. One day Dr. L. O. Dawson, our
Bible teacher, complimented Frances for getting her college education along with her husband. He urged her to continue in school
as long as I did. I assured him that she would, adding, "You
see, I am a model husband." With a sly grin he replied, "Yes, I
am sure that you are. The dictionary defines a 'model' as a fair
imitation of the real thing." I relate this not only to show how
he put me in my place, but also to stress the need for training
on the part of a preacher's wife.

I majored in Bible in college. In fact, they had to form such a "major" by combining with the normal courses in Bible required of all students such subjects as Greek, church history, and religious education.

I was preparing for the ministry. It did not occur to me at the time that these fields would be covered more in depth in the seminary. Looking back, I came to learn that it would have been better had I majored in some other field: English, history, education, psychology, or one of the sciences. I state this simply to be helpful to others. You should seek to cover broader fields of knowledge in college, leaving the specialized religious courses for the seminary. Of course, if you do not plan to attend a seminary, the course I took would prove helpful.

Why this broader major? Because it will familiarize you with other areas of knowledge than religion. You will find that in preaching you will or should make the Bible central. But a knowledge of other fields will enable you to draw from them illustrative material for the purpose of clarifying biblical truth and relating it to life. Often among your listeners there will be those related to these broader fields. Showing that you are at home in them will gain from such people both respect and attention. It will give them a sense of confidence in you. If you are knowledgeable in their fields, they will conclude that you certainly are at home in yours.

Apart from the major field, in college you should take in-depth studies in other courses. Psychology will help you in understanding the human mind and spirit. Knowledge of the sciences will enable you better to relate biblical truth with modern thought. Courses in literature will provide a gold mine of material for illustrations. A working knowledge of Latin, Greek, German, and the Romance languages will enable you better to understand the English tongue.

During graduate work in the seminary I taught a class in basic English grammar for first-year students who make less than seventy on a placement examination. One student, upon learning that he must take the course, was upset. Said he, "This is ridiculous! I majored in English in college!" I replied, "Well, you may be able to quote Byron, Keats, Shakespeare, and Shelley by the hour; but you cannot diagram a simple sentence." Since English is one of the tools of your trade, you should be well grounded in it.

At the seminary I took the full Master in Theology (standard degree at the time) course. During this time Mrs. Hobbs studied at both the seminary and Woman's Missionary Training School. Following this degree I continued until I received the Doctor of Philosophy degree, majoring in New Testament interpretation. I state the latter simply to show my disagreement with those who hold that one should take the doctorate degree only if he plans to teach. If a pastor is so disposed, why should he not also receive the thorough training involved? The people in the pew need teaching as well as those in a college or seminary classroom.

Returning to the idea of a college major, it is of interest to note that in the doctoral work in New Testament a proportionate share of the study dealt with ancient history. The Bible was not produced in a vacuum but was wrought out in the hot fires of the history of the era. Knowledge of ancient history contemporary with any part of the Bible is necessary to its understanding on your part. Had I majored in ancient history in college, I would have been better prepared for this advanced study of the New Testament.

My purpose in this brief autobiographical statement is to stress the possibility of your receiving college and seminary training. There are denominational colleges and/or state-supported colleges and universities located in every part of the nation which are available to those who desire to pursue higher education. Southern Baptists alone have six strategically located seminaries. In addition, there are many other such schools. Even if you cannot be a full-time, on-campus student, you can arrange with your church to commute for as much work as possible. I know of one pastor of a full-time church in a city where one of our seminaries is located. He took as many courses as his schedule would allow. It required many years to finish the required work, but he continued until he received his degree.

As suggested above, for some of you even this may not be possible. You may have entered the ministry later in life. Because of age and family responsibilities you may not feel that you can give the time for four years in college and three more years in the seminary. But there is no reason why you cannot take advantage of available opportunities. You can study your Bible, using commentaries and other books to guide you. You can take advantage of study offered at Bible conferences and encampments. Many colleges offer night extension courses taught by faculty members or other qualified teachers. The six Southern Baptist seminaries cooperate in a well-organized seminary extension program. Textbooks and courses of study written by capable scholars are provided to meet the needs of those who have achieved various educational levels. A God-called preacher should take advantage of the educational opportunities available to him.

In all honesty, however, we should recognize that there are areas of service where a pastor with limited academic achievements can serve more effectively than one who is highly educated. A high school or college graduate with training through the seminary extension program may meet the spiritual needs of a given congregation better than one who has a Ph.D. The reverse will also be true in other pastorates. Nevertheless, it should be recognized that the intellectual and academic level even in rural areas is far higher than it was a generation ago. God has a place for every servant and a servant for every place. And he expects each of us to prepare to the limit of our ability and opportunity in both mind and spirit for maximum service for him.

Matter of Attitude

It is not the size of the dog in the fight but the size of the fight in the dog that counts. This is a homey way of saying that for you as a preacher, success in both training and service is governed by your attitude. Even time spent in the seminary may largely be wasted if you approach it with the wrong attitude.

At the beginning of my second year in the seminary a first-year student enrolled. He was a handsome young man with a good personality. Those who heard him said that he was a good pulpiteer. He was soon called to a good church in the city, while most of us were happy to have the small country or village churches far removed from the campus. This man had the innate qualities designed to make him a powerful and successful pastor—except one. He had the wrong attitude. It was reported to me that he said, "They can't teach me anything here. I only came to the seminary for the prestige it will give me." Consequently, he gave very little time and effort to his studies. It was not long before he dropped out of school. I have not heard of him since. I believe I know Southern Baptist pastors fairly well. But to save my life I cannot tell you where he is or what he had done. It all began with an improper attitude.

You should remember that teachers do not *learn* you, they *teach* you. The learning is up to you. Alexander Pope said, "Some people never learn anything because they understand everything too soon." Or they think they do. There is a sermon for every preacher in the words of Seneca. "As the soil, however rich it may be, cannot be productive without culture, so the mind without cultivation can never produce good fruits." Someone said that the price of mastery in any field is thorough preparation.

It was my privilege to be taught by some of the "giants"— Carver, Davis, Dobbins, Robertson, Sampey, and Yates—to name only a few. But despite the volume of knowledge they tried to impart to me, in the long haul they taught me more by what they were than by what they said. They were dedicated to the task of preparing young preachers for their ministry. And they did everything within their power, even to being rough on us at times, to accomplish their mission. Of interest is the fact that when a group of my contemporaries gets together to recall seminary experiences, we always talk with appreciation for those who were hardest on us. What was at the time bitter medicine has become as sweet as honey with the passing of the years.

Education does not give you all the facts, but it teaches you to study. It does not provide all the answers. But it does enable you to ask intelligent questions and to find the answers. Someone defined an educated person not as the one who knows the most, but as the one who knows how and where to find the answers to life's questions. In the few short years spent in getting an education, you do not receive *pat* answers to the problems of life. Instead, you develop the discipline and skill to seek their solution for yourself and others.

Henry Ward Beecher said, "Education is the knowledge of how to use the whole of one's self. Many men use but one or two faculties out of the score with which they are endowed. A man is educated who knows how to make a tool of every faculty— how to open it, how to keep it sharp, and how to apply it to all practical purposes." Tryon Edwards reminds us that "the great end of education is to discipline rather than to furnish the mind; to train it to the use of its own powers, rather than to fill it with the accumulation of others."

Ponder long the words of Joseph Addison. "What sculpture is to a block of marble, education is to the human soul. The philosopher, the saint, the hero, the wise and the good, or the great, very often lie hid and concealed in a plebeian, which a proper education might have disinterred and brought to light."

Fried Chicken or a Bad Egg

Never will I forget a story told by the speaker at a seminary luncheon for my graduating class as we were inducted into the alumni group. He began his message by portraying a scene familiar to every preacher. He imagined us as being a guest in a home for the Sunday noon meal. In the middle of the table is a platter filled with mouth-watering fried chicken. Then he asked this question. "Did it ever occur to you that the difference between that fried chicken and its being a bad egg was the incubator that hatched the egg?" He applied the story by likening the seminary, our alma mater, to the incubator.

Happy is the preacher who can look to some seminary as his alma mater. However, according to the situation it may be a college, an extension study program, or even home study on your own. The fact remains that the difference between your being "fried chicken" or a "bad egg" is the way you apply yourself in developing your *tools* and *skills* through study. (I am assuming that you will by God's grace develop your spiritual condition.)

To be the kind of preacher God called you to be is not easy. It calls for arduous toil, brain sweat, and rigorous discipline. God never does through a miracle what he can do through a man. Even Jesus, as he identified himself with man, apart from sin, had to learn to walk, talk, master the Scriptures, and fulfill his destiny as the Suffering Servant of God. You can expect no easier way to fill the role God has designed for you.

Stewardship involves more than money. It encompasses all that you have and are. You cannot preach stewardship of life to others unless you first demonstrate it to them, any more than you can effectively preach tithing to your people if they know that you do not tithe. So, physician, heal yourself before you try to treat others!

In a very real sense you are *becoming* what you *are*. If you are a know-it-all now, you will be one throughout life—unless someone takes the wind out of your sails. If you loaf in school, you will loaf on the job. A cheat in school will be a cheat in life. If you try to take shortcuts now you will do so in your work—and wind up in the blind alley of frustration and failure.

One of my classmates in the seminary was a man who was older than the rest of us. He had a handsome physique and a wonderful speaking voice. His slightly gray hair gave him a distinguished appearance. And he had two good sermons which he used when preaching at a church in view of a call. But he would not study. He was lazy in both mind and body. So, once called, he had little else to offer the church. When called upon to recite, he tried to bluff his way through. Usually the teacher, trying to prime his pump, would start the answer to a question. The man would repeat that, but nothing more could he say.

At that time "Amos and Andy" was the most popular radio show. Andy was an ignorant blowhard. When someone would say something, without understanding a word of it he would say, "Sho!" So a friend of mine and I gave this man the nickname "Sho." One day in Greek class he was called upon to recite. Since he sat across the aisle from me, he stood beside me to recite. In the professor's absence the fellow was teaching. He asked this man to read from the Greek New Testament. Unable to do so, the fellow read the first word. He repeated it. After several words the fellow said, "Brother Blank, I have shown that I can read it. Now suppose you try. What is the next word?" During the long silence over my shoulder to my friend behind me I whispered, "Sho." The poor man heard it. Thinking I was prompting him, he blurted out "It means 'sho!' " The fellow promptly sat him down. Years later I told the fellow this story. He said, "You know, ever since then I've been trying to figure out how he got that translation."

During the following years this man drifted from pastorate to pastorate. Eventually he became a chaplain in the federal prison. The last report I had on him, he was an inmate of it. He had been convicted of raising the figure on his paycheck. So much ability wasted! So tragic an end! And all because of a wrong attitude.

Some years ago a traveler was on a muddy country road. Finally he came to a sign which read, "Be careful which rut you get in, for you will be in it for the next ten miles."

Watch out for the beginnings. Check your attitude in light of God's will. The road ahead may not be easy. But he who called you will go with you. Often the only way *out* of a situation is *through it.*

In one verse Luke summed up eighteen years of Jesus' life. "And Jesus increased in wisdom and stature, and in favour with

God and man" (2:52). The verb "increased" uses a tense which means that he kept on doing this. He began and continued to do so. It means to cut one's way forward as through a jungle. Keep in mind that Jesus did this in his humanity. He kept cutting his way forward as he grew in wisdom, in stature or size, and in favor with God and man.

We do not do harm to this verse as we apply it to ourselves. You as a preacher should begin and continue to cut your way forward through the jungle toward growing knowledge. The word rendered "stature" clearly means physical size in Jesus' case as he grew from a boy into a man. But the same word is used for length and/or quality of life. In your case it can mean that you rise in stature as God's servant. Doing this, you will also be regarded with favor by both God and man—the one whom you serve and those to whom you minister.

If you are to make the desired progress through the jungle, you must continue to keep your blade sharp through a discipline of study beyond seminary days. You will do this as you begin and continue to develop your mental and spiritual faculties. Education is something you begin in time. But it should never end until God calls you up higher.

4

Whither, Lord?

Dr. George W. Truett once said, "Most preachers are like Abraham. They looketh for a field." Of course, in this sense "field" means a pastorate.

In January of my first year in the seminary a classmate from Alabama received word that his father, who was a farmer, had broken his leg. It was necessary for him to return home to "make a crop." Dr. W. O. Carver heard about his leaving school, but did not know the reason for it. One day he met this student on the campus and mentioned the matter to him. Then he asked, "Do you have a *field* back in Alabama?" The student said that he did. Telling me about it, he grinned and said, "But I did not tell him that a mule would be my assistant pastor."

But seriously, the matter of where you are to serve the Lord is of the greatest importance. This is true whether it be your first pastorate after your seminary days or other pastorates in the future. Having sharpened your axe, you are now ready to be led to the place where all your effort and time will be given to pastoral ministry. And as Paul asked, "What shall I do, Lord?" (Acts 22:10), so you should ask, "Where shall I do it, Lord?" If you listen carefully, you will find the truth of the promise given in the remainder of the verse. "It shall be told thee of all things which are appointed for thee to do."

Instruments of God

As I believe that God calls men into the ministry, so I believe that he is able and willing to place them where they are to serve.

For this reason you should not try to run ahead of him. That you should make it a matter of prayer is quite evident. You should not pray that God will give you a certain church but that he will place you where he wants you to be.

And God has many instruments through which your prayers may be answered—or, to use a better word—granted. The seminary itself is such an instrument. I am sure that it receives many requests from churches for recommendation of a prospective pastor. The state Baptist convention workers are other instruments. Churches in a given state more often than not turn to them for guidance. Most state Baptist papers each year publish a list of those from that state who are graduating from the seminary. There is nothing wrong in your writing to the executive secretary of your state to let him know that you are available—or, for that matter, in writing the same information to your home-church pastor or other friends. However, you should not limit the Holy Spirit's leadership by refusing to go elsewhere if he wills.

You should not turn aside from opportunities which present themselves while you wait for a certain kind of church of your choosing to call you. You want to be where God wills you to be, not simply where you want to be. He may will that you spend some time being *seasoned* in a lesser place before moving up higher. You should take to heart the lesson in Jesus' parable of the dinner guests. It is better to take a lesser seat and then be invited to move up higher than to sit at the head table, only to be asked later to take a lower seat.

Someone said that the man who never made a mistake is working for someone who did. Being human, you will make mistakes— not only at the beginning but throughout your ministry. It is better to make some of them in a less pretentious place before you become established in your ministry than to do so in a more prominent place.

Two years after I finished the seminary a friend told me that he had recommended me to the First Baptist Church, Oklahoma City. I knew that they would not consider me. But in my heart

I felt that had they called me, I could have done the job. I now know that it would have been tragic for them and for me. Ten years later the pulpit committee from that church visited me. Kidding them, I asked, "What took you so long?" They asked what I meant. I told them that I knew that ten years before I had been recommended to them. After we had laughed about it, one man said that at that time he was secretary of the pulpit committee. When my name came up for consideration—after ten years—he recalled the letter and read it to the present committee. By that time I had seasoned somewhat. It was the beginning of a happy pastorate of almost twenty-four years.

When W. A. Criswell finished his doctoral work at Southern Baptist Theological Seminary, two churches were considering him. One was the First Baptist Church in a large Southern city. The other was the First Baptist Church, Chickasha, Oklahoma, a nice but much smaller city. W. A. and his wife, Betty, had agreed that the first one to call him would be to them the Lord's will. The church in Chickasha called, and they accepted. Only a few days later a call came from the other church. Being human, at first they felt a sense of disappointment. But, true to their word, they went to Chickasha. After a happy pastorate there they went to the First Baptist Church, Muskogee, Oklahoma. It was from there that they went to First Baptist Church, Dallas, Texas. Looking back, they could see God's hand as he prepared them for their greatest challenge—one which they have met gloriously.

Incidentally, it was while Dr. Criswell was pastor of a small country church near Bowling Green, Kentucky, that Dr. John L. Hill of the Sunday School Board of the Southern Baptist Convention heard him preach. Later he recommended him to the church in the large city mentioned above. Several years later, after the *seasoning* process, the First Baptist Church, Dallas, asked Dr. Hill for a recommendation. He replied that W. A. Criswell was their man. The rest is history.

A humorous note was sounded shortly after Dr. Criswell's call to Dallas. Dr. J. W. Storer, First Baptist Church, Tulsa, Oklahoma, was a master at satire. A newspaper story said that Dr. Criswell was chosen out of a list of sixty-five pastors who were considered. Dr. Storer wrote an article which appeared in the state Baptist papers. He pictured the sixty-four comparing their abilities with Dr. Criswell's. Finally, one asked, "Well what does this young man have that we do not have?" In unison the others replied, "The call!"

The point is that God did it through human instruments. For years the question was asked, "Who will succeed Dr. Truett?" God knew. And in ways of his own choosing he was preparing his man for his place. You should be willing to wait on the Lord. If you remain in God's will, the man, the place, and the hour will meet—in the fullness of time.

Errors to Avoid

At this point let us take the longer look. You are located in a pastorate. But the impression comes that you should move to another field of service. Someone said that preachers move for one of two reasons—the *call* of the Lord or the *push* of brethren. I know of no situation so unhappy as a pastor who feels that he should move and a church which shares that feeling—but no opportunity is open to him. Thus the situation becomes an endurance contest.

But before moving further into this matter, a word is in order to the members of a church. The following idea is not original with me. But I will endeavor to express it in my own words.

"Brother Layman, so you want a new pastor. Let me tell you how to get one. Start going to all services—Sunday morning, Sunday night, and Wednesday night. Accept places of responsibility in the church, and fulfill them to the best of your ability. Stop criticizing your pastor for his weak points and mistakes. Instead, pick out his good points and brag on them to his face and to other people. See that he and his family are properly provided for in a material way. *Pray for* him; do not *prey on* him. Push forward instead of pulling back. Enlarge the scope of your vision. Dream big dreams with your pastor, and labor to make them a reality. Counsel with him and bolster him with the skills of your own vocation. Enlist others to do the same. And you will get a new pastor. He will be the same man you now have. But he will be a new and better pastor."

When I was pastor of the Dauphin Way Baptist Church, Mobile, Alabama, one of the deacons was Will Milling. Once each week he came by to see me. He would say, "Pastor, I do not want anything. I just came by to pray with you." He was a constant tower of strength to his pastor.

But now let us look at some errors to avoid with respect to a prospective change of pastorates. One error is to see the grass as being greener in some new field. I have known a few pastors who were always restless. No sooner did they move to a new field but they started looking for another—and always one that was *bigger* and *better*. Such rolling stones gather no moss where they are or elsewhere.

Again, some preachers in a crisis situation resign in a fit of anger—*with no place to go.* Therefore, as a result it is extremely hard for them to receive a call elsewhere. Pulpit committees wonder why such a preacher does not have a pastorate. Often when hearing of such I have remarked to friends, "If you hear that I have done that, just know that it is a false report. I may get angry, but not to that degree."

Perhaps the greatest error to be avoided is the manner used by some preachers in getting their names before pastorless churches. It both degrades the ministry and lessens your chances of being given serious consideration by a pulpit committee. This error consists of writing a large number of other pastors—some close friends, and others mere acquaintances—asking that they recommend you to a given church. More often than not, you may be totally unfitted for the church in view. But just suppose that all of them do as you request. A pulpit committee deluged with so many letters will recognize at once that it is the result of a *campaign.*

Unless you are closely connected with a person, you should not ask him for such a letter. Furthermore, you should not abuse friendships. It would be far better to let friends know of your situation and to leave them free to write on your behalf as each feels led to do so. It is one thing to be your friend and another to know your strengths and weaknesses. If you specify a church, he may feel that you are not suited for it. Yet out of friendship he may write a letter at your request. This could actually be a harmful act if it results in your being in a pastorate with which you cannot cope. You will soon be asking for another such *favor*. And it is unfair to you and to the church.

I heard of one preacher who responded to such requests unwillingly, but in a manner designed to pull his punches. He would always close his letters thus. "When you know Rev. John Doe as I know him, you will feel toward him as I do." Wise pulpit committees could easily read between the lines and file the letter in the wastebasket.

Now just a word to those who are requested to write such letters. You should not handle the truth recklessly. Whatever you write should be true and positive. But some things should be left unsaid. Do not write a glowing letter when you know that one is not justified. *You should be fair with the church to which you write.* For the past twenty years I have noticed that fewer pulpit committees are requesting recommendations from pastors. In response to a question as to why this is the case, one committee chairman told me, "It is because pastors in an effort to be nice do not give all the facts in the case." This is to our shame. It might be well to give some adverse information where justified— with an explanation as to why certain conditions arose. In many cases the pastor is the victim rather than the creator of circumstances.

Several years ago a committee from the trustees of a large university spent two hours in my home talking about a friend of mine as a prospective president. In a previous presidency there had been problems. I was in a position to know all the facts. So I decided to lay the entire situation on the table—showing where he had been at fault and where he was the victim of others. Before the interview closed I told the committee that I felt that the man under consideration had learned much from the entire experience and that because of it he would make them a good president.

Later he was elected to that presidency. The committee chairman wrote to thank me for my help. He said that they knew of the problems but not about all the circumstances. He then added that had I tried to cover up or gloss over the matter, they would have dropped his name from further consideration. But due to my frankness, they pursued the matter to their satisfaction and recommended his election.

If you write a letter concerning another pastor, by all means do not say that the Holy Spirit is leading you to do so unless you honestly feel that he is! In the familiar story of Ananias, Peter said, "Ananias, why hast Satan filled thine heart to lie to the Holy Ghost [Spirit]?" (Acts 5:3). The Greek text reads "to falsify the Holy Spirit." In other words, he included the Holy Spirit as a partner in his dishonest act. Before including the Holy Spirit in such a letter, you should read and reread this story. It is a terrible sin to include the Holy Spirit in your act unless you honestly feel his leadership.

During my seminary days a group of students conducted chapel services one day in which they dealt with the ethics of seeking a pastorate. I have never forgotten a story related by one. The chairman of the pulpit committee of a small rural church in southern Kentucky told him of receiving over a hundred letters of recommendation for different men. Some were even written by the men themselves. Every writer of a letter said that he was writing under the leadership of the Holy Spirit. Would the Holy Spirit be so confused and/or confusing? Then the man said, "Preacher, between some Baptist preachers and the 'Holy Rollers,' the Holy Spirit is getting a bad deal in Southern Kentucky!" No further comment is necessary.

Proper Procedure

Perhaps I am not qualified out of personal experience to write about this. By the grace of God and the goodness of the brethren, I have never needed to seek a pastorate. The nearest I ever came to doing it was just prior to entering my doctoral studies at the seminary. At the time I was pastor of two half-time churches in Indiana. Due to the cost of travel, the income was insufficient for the cost of living. A professor had asked me to serve as his fellow. The job paid thirty-five dollars per month, the amount needed to meet the need. But the man who was occupying that fellowship was at the last minute asked to remain as an instructor following graduation. To supplement his salary, he continued to serve as fellow for one more year. Of course, that left me high and dry.

Mrs. Hobbs and I had moved to our church field for the summer, but continued to make this a matter of prayer. Since we saw no way to finance further study on our present financial basis, I wrote my major professor, Dr. W. Hersey Davis, to let him know my situation. Unless I could get work nearer Louisville, I could not pursue my plans to study for the doctorate. Following that letter I had agreed to preach with view to a call at a smalltown church in Alabama.

The day before we were to leave for Alabama I received three letters—two from Dr. Davis and one from Dr. J. B. Weatherspoon, professor of homiletics and sociology. I opened them in the order of the dates they were postmarked. In the first one Dr. Davis told me he knew of no available work. The second said that he had just met Dr. Weatherspoon in the hall, who had the previous day returned from a trip to the Orient. Needing a fellow, he asked Dr. Davis to suggest someone. He said that he gave him my name, but that I should not write him unless he first wrote me. The third letter was from Dr. Weatherspoon, inviting me to be his fellow. Of course, I accepted and I notified the church in Alabama of the new development, saying that it would be unwise for me to preach for them. The Lord solved our problems in an unexpected way.

However, observation and religious common sense tell us some things. For whatever reason you may feel that you should change pastorates, certain ethical and spiritual things are obvious. Everything you do should be bathed in prayer. It should be permeated with "not what I will, but what thou wilt" (Mark 14:36).

If you come to the place where you feel that you should move to another pastorate, certainly you should talk to the Lord about it. If Gideon put out his fleeces, why should you not do the same? If you do so in prayer and trust, God will reveal his will to you. It may be to go or to stay. He will either open or shut doors. But you must be open to do his will in either case.

Many years ago the First Baptist Church in a large Southern city approached me about considering a call to become its pastor. I did not feel led to do so. After several refusals by phone and mail, a subcommittee of the pulpit committee visited me. They assured me that they would not accept a negative answer until I visited their church. I did so the following week. All of my dealings were with the subcommittee which wanted to recommend me to the full committee. I insisted that they had no assurance that the larger group would accept their recommendation. On Thursday I returned home with the understanding that if any new development came on either end of the line, the other would be notified.

After worship services the following Sunday morning Mrs. Hobbs' mother suggested that we put out a fleece. If I did not hear from them by midnight, we were to remain where we were. We agreed. That night I awoke and looked at the clock by my bed. It was 12:25 A.M. We were not to go. Early the next morning I sent a telegram to that effect. Later that morning I received a call from the committee chairman expressing his regrets. The previous afternoon the full committee had voted unanimously to recommend that the church extend me a call. Had the chairman called me immediately, as agreed, they would have had a pastor.

As it was, we spent several more happy years where we were.

The "fleece" idea also works the other way. Early in Billy Graham's rise to fame as an evangelist, a group of pastors asked me to join them in inviting him to hold a crusade in Oklahoma City. I was hesitant to do so, since I was not certain at that time as to his attitude toward the local church. It was not long before he knew about this. About a year later I was satisfied on this matter. So a group of us at my request extended the invitation. Time passed with no acceptance. In July of that year (1955) Mrs. Hobbs and I were with a party touring Europe and the Middle East. We were in Lucerne, Switzerland, where, unknown to us, Billy and his team were resting between crusades. Hearing that a group of Baptists were in the city, they came and ate dinner with us. During the meal I went to his table and told him I was praying that he would come for the crusade. Shortly thereafter he accepted.

The next year when he arrived in Oklahoma City, a news reporter asked when he knew it was God's will that he come. He said, "It was when Dr. Herschel Hobbs came to my table in Lucerne, saying that he was praying that I would come. I had put out fleeces to determine the Lord's will. All but one had come back with an affirmative answer. The last fleece was that Dr. Hobbs would personally invite me." Little did I know at the time the significance of that brief word with him in Lucerne.

God never does through a miracle what he can do through a human being. Earlier I mentioned the idea of communicating your feelings to friends in position to help. You should do that—and nothing more—except to pray for God's will to be done.

One of the best pieces of advice I ever heard in this regard came from my Bible professor in college. A ministerial student asked that he recommend him to another church. He said, "Now you just build a big fire where you are. Somebody will see the smoke and come over to investigate it."

Through the years I have followed a very simple rule which I have shared with staff members. Never leave a place until you feel as strongly led from it as you felt led to it. Problems will arise wherever you deal with people. It will be a great source of comfort, patience, and strength to know that in your pastorate you are in the center of God's will.

One final word needs to be said at this point. Let us suppose that you and a pulpit committee agree that God is leading you to become the pastor of their church. There should be a clear understanding as to the agreement reached. It may include such matters as salary, housing, retirement plan, moving expenses, staff, vacation, time allowed for absences for revivals and the like, expenses for conventions, and/or other matters. One of the soundest pieces of advice in this regard ever given his students by Dr. Gaines S. Dobbins was to get all this in writing. It protects both the church and pastor from later misunderstandings.

God, an Administrator

One day a cynical person said to me, "It is strange to me that when a preacher says it is God's will that he move, it is always to a larger church with an increase in salary." My reply went something like this.

"You are a businessman heading a large corporation which employs many hundreds of people. As such you are its administrative head. Now is it not true that when you find a promising young man, you place him in a lesser position in your organization with a corresponding salary? If he proves himself there, is it not also true that you promote him to a more important position with greater responsibility? And do you not increase his salary in keeping with his new position and the higher standard of living his new work demands? This process is repeated over and over again. Eventually he may rise to the highest echelon in the corporation with a commensurate income. Is not all of this true?" He nodded his assent.

I continued, "Well, God is an infinitely greater and wiser administrator than you. So, likewise, he places a young minister of promise in a small church with a corresponding salary. Once he proves himself there, God leads him to a larger work with increased responsibility. This process continues in an ever upward scale. And each time he moves upward he receives an increase in salary, in keeping with his greater responsibility and higher standard of living. So, you see, God promotes his men as you do yours. At the same time many people willingly take a reduction in salary to answer God's call to teach in a college or a seminary or to become a missionary. How many of your employees have voluntarily done a similar thing?" He could name none.

When a person enlists in the military and takes the oath of allegiance, actually he has made his last decision on his own. Thereafter he is under orders. This is also true of one who responds to God's call into the ministry. Of his own will he submits to God's will. From that time on he has but one overall question to ask. "What shall I do, Lord?" This applies not only to his work but where he will do it. If he wills that you serve in a lowly place as the world judges, so be it. If he has other plans for you, so be it.

I have had preachers say to me, "I am just a little pastor of a little church." No pastor or church is little unless he/it chooses to be. Many churches small in numbers are great in spirit. Others large in numbers may be small in spirit. And many pastors in the former churches are doing a greater work for the Lord than others in the latter churches. Wherever you are, do your best for the Lord; and leave these other matters with him.

The story is told of a young minister who asked the Duke of Wellington how he could succeed in the ministry. "What are your marching orders?" asked the Duke. The young man quoted to him the Great Commission. Then the Duke asked, "Well, young man, what are you waiting for?" Amen! And Amen!

5

Pastor or Potentate?

One day Mrs. Hobbs and I were discussing something we would like to see accomplished in our church. Hearing us, our seven-year-old son asked, "Well, Daddy, aren't you the boss at the church? Why don't you just tell them to do it?" The thought went through my mind, *Oh, son, if you only knew!*

There is no place for a "boss" in a New Testament church. Leaders and followers? Yes. But bosses and servants? No. If you as a pastor do not recognize this, you are headed for trouble—of your own making.

Pastor's Peculiar Position

Except when a man goes into business for himself, the only two people I know who start out at the top are a pastor and a well digger. It is at this very point that you as a pastor are in a peculiar position. As such you bear responsibility without authority. In one sense you are the administrative head of the church. The congregation determines policy, and under its authority you administer it. Your actions are subject to review by the church body, and often by that of each self-appointed critic within the church fellowship.

The only *authority* you possess is that of leadership and example. Unlike the centurion you cannot say, "Go, and he goeth . . . Come, and he cometh . . . Do this, and he doeth it" (Matt. 8:9). And yet, under such circumstances you are expected to produce results. You are called upon to lead the greatest of voluntary work forces. Still your leadership will be no more effective than the followship of your people. At times you may be tempted to assume authority because no one else will. You may try to push and shove rather than to lead. When you do, you set yourself up as the target of barbs of criticism—usually hurled the most by those who do nothing else. But even this may hinder the work and eventually harm your ministry, maybe destroy its effectiveness entirely.

Thus you are called upon to walk the tightrope between being responsible and at the same time not being domineering. The early apostles apparently possessed apostolic authority which was not passed on to others. At the same time you have only to read Paul's writings to see how hesitant he was to assert that power. Peter wrote to "the elders which are among you, I exhort, who am also an elder" (1 Pet. 5:1). The Greek word rendered "elder" means "fellow elder." He was a fellow elder, not a super elder. Both Paul and Peter *exhorted,* but seldom *ordered* (Eph. 4:1; 1 Pet. 5:1).

Suggested Procedure

As a pastor you must distinguish between firm, positive leadership and an effort to exercise authority. Before embarking on any undertaking you should seek to know God's will in the matter. Yet you should also recognize that you alone do not have a private pipeline to God. For this reason there is value in the counsel of others—your staff and/or other dedicated leaders in the congregation. Through the sharing of ideas and dreams, and through personal and corporate prayer, God will reveal his will. The more people you involve in the formulative process, the more enthusiasm they will have to join in seeing the program through to a successful conclusion. And only after thus praying and thinking through a proposed endeavor are you ready to reveal it to your people as a whole.

A wise military strategist who leads his forces through strange territory will scout ahead for possible opposition. As a wise pastor you also should seek to anticipate areas of resistance and should endeavor to gain their cooperation. Furthermore, you should not present any proposed program to responsible groups within the church until you are reasonably certain that it will be approved. You should never *slip up* on your people. We are so constituted that we tend to resist that which we do not understand. This is true whether it be a local congregation or a larger denominational body. At the same time people tend to respond favorably to that which they understand. It is true that adequate information is necessary for people to give intelligent cooperation.

It has been my experience that if, in presenting a matter, you give evidence of having done your homework and have all of your *ducks in a row,* it will be accepted. But if one *duck* is not in line, someone will take a potshot at it.

On one occasion our deacons appointed a committee to study the matter of erecting a new building for one of our missions. After several meetings it felt that it was ready to report. Preliminary plans for the building and cost estimates had been obtained. I raised the question of how to finance it. The group agreed that this matter could come later. Against my better judgment I went along with them. At a called meeting of the deacons the report was presented. The first question asked was regarding finances. When the committee chairman said that this had not been determined, the questioner said, "I move that we adjourn and meet at such time the committee is ready with a full report." At a later meeting when the full report was presented, the program was unanimously recommended to the church.

There are times when it is wise to wait rather than to ride roughshod over opposition. Many years ago T. L. Holcomb told me of an experience he had when he was a pastor. The church wanted to build an educational building. When the matter was being considered by the deacons, all but one man favored it. This man was one of influence and financial means, but he was opposed to the necessary debt involved. Dr. Holcomb said that he could have pushed the matter, and the church would have adopted it. But in doing so they could have lost the cooperation of an able, conscientious man. So he suggested that the program be delayed. Six months later this man came to him. "Pastor," said he, "I was wrong in opposing the building program. I have come to request that we go ahead with it. And I want to be made chairman of a committee to raise the money for it." By waiting six months they got the building and the wholehearted cooperation of the entire congregation.

Speaking of running roughshod over people, you may by so doing win some battles but lose the war. Each time you win such a battle you will leave behind you little pockets of opposition. In some crisis these groups may get together and become a formidable force with which you cannot cope. In military life the term *mopping up* is used—meaning to destroy such resistance before moving ahead. But in church life it is wise to win full cooperation so that no pockets of resistance arise. This will require patience and tact, to be sure. It may call for compromise where no moral principle is involved. Any leader is wise to weigh the evidence involved in differences of opinion. Usually there are some values in all sides of a question. One purpose in debate is to refine the ore of conflicting opinions to arrive at the gold of truth. You should never seek simply to get your way in a matter, but to find God's way and then proceed with unity. This process may cause delay in the program, but it will mean a better one in the long run.

Of course, you may face a situation in which you cannot find a meeting ground with some people. Such may be born in the *objective* case and the *kickative* mode and argue for the sake of argument. After all reasonable efforts have been made to refine truth and to secure their cooperation in what the church wishes to do, only to fail, then the church must proceed with what it deems to be God's will. The matter of such people you must leave in the hands of the Lord.

It is wise for a church to have a constitution and bylaws. With such, if a crisis arises it can be handled on the basis of principles rather than personalities. This provides a means by which you as the pastor may lead the people in resolving problems. By all means you as the pastor should avoid debating issues. In most instances you are the moderator of the church. A moderator should never take sides. It is his responsibility to provide a firm but fair hand in guiding the proceedings. Once you take sides you will lose your opposition completely.

During almost a half-century as a pastor I have observed that church members can enter into heated debate without leaving scars. But if the pastor becomes involved, those opposing his position take it as a personal affront. Nowhere does the phrase "wise as serpents and harmless as doves" (Matt. 10:16) apply more than in the pastor's efforts to lead his people through the disagreements of good, honest people with respect to the activities of the church. Even by parliamentary law the moderator is forbidden any action which sways a debated issue either way. Following this provision not only will protect your position as pastor; it also leaves the body free of coercion as in true democratic procedure it decides the issue. If you feel compelled to speak you should surrender the gavel to someone else, and not take it back again until after the issue is decided. But it is far better for you to keep the gavel and let the matter be determined on its merits. If a proposal cannot stand up under debate, it should be dropped altogether.

Multiple Role of Ministers

An effective ministry calls for an understanding as to the role of the minister—understanding on his part and on the part of his people. In popular modern Christian terminology the words *elder, bishop,* and *pastor* are used to refer to different offices or groups of people. "Elder" in some circles is used of an office equivalent to that of "deacon." "Bishop" likewise refers to one who is over a group of churches such as a diocese or a conference. "Pastor," of course, denotes one who serves in a local church.

However, this is not true of the uses in the New Testament, where different phases of the same office are referred to. This is most evident in Acts 20:28, which involves all three concepts but relates them to the same people. "Take heed therefore unto yourselves, and to all the flock, over the which the Holy Ghost (Spirit) hath made you overseers, to feed the church of God, which he hath purchased with his own blood."

Note that these words were spoken to the "elders of the church" in Ephesus (Acts 20:17). These elders are "overseers." And they are "to feed" the church of God. "Elders" translates a Greek word *presbuterous* (note "Presbyterian"). "Overseers" renders *episkopous* (note "Episcopal"). "To feed" translates a word meaning to serve as a shepherd. Since this was pastoral work, from this verb comes the word "pastor."

Among the Jews an elder was a person of great age whose experience and wisdom enabled him to give wise counsel. But in the Christian sense the emphasis is less upon age and more upon giving counsel. The word "overseer" among the Greeks referred to a person who oversaw the work of others to be sure that they did it correctly. In the Christian sense this word is translated as *bishop* (Phil. 1:1; 1 Tim. 3:1). It is never used of one over a group of churches. Thus in the New Testament sense every church has its own *bishop*. Since the Philippian letter was addressed to "the bishops and deacons" (1:1), it shows that some churches had a plurality of bishops. This same plurality is evident in "the elders of the church" (Acts 20:17) and "bishops" (Acts 20:28) with reference to the church in Ephesus. Probably such churches had a senior elder/bishop under whose direction others served.

To serve as a shepherd connoted all the duties of a shepherd in caring for his flock such as feeding, leading, protecting, and treating the ill and wounded. The noun form of this word is used in the Christian sense as *pastor* (Eph. 4:11). Thus from this one verse you see the multiple role of the minister. He is to be *counselor, overseer,* and *shepherd.*

Every pastor knows the demanding role of being a counselor. And in our pressure-cooker age it is involving more and more of the pastor's time and energy. It is unnecessary to list the many areas touched by this need. Indeed, they will differ from pastorate to pastorate. My generation of preachers had to learn by main strength and awkwardness how to fill this role. Happily, seminaries now provide intensive study in this field. However, one word of caution is needed. Simply because you have studied these courses, do not think that you are qualified as a psychiatrist. When such treatment is needed, you should refer a person to a Christian psychiatrist. Unfortunately, many psychiatrists seem to regard people as they would animals. They treat only natural functions of the body with little or no regard for the spiritual element. This is why I used the term "Christian psychiatrist," or one who takes into account man's spiritual self. Such can be found. But you must look for them.

The matter of reference is true of any other specialized field. Physicians often refer patients to specialists. Why should not pastors do the same? It may be that a person needs to see a medical doctor, a financial consultant, or a lawyer—as the case may be. It is far better for you to admit your limitations than to give someone the wrong advice. No one person is an expert in all fields. It is not to your shame but to your credit if you recognize this and are guided thereby. You should no more seek to give legal advice than to perform a surgical operation. Stick to your field and utilize the skills of others. I have found that where I personally made the initial contact with the specialist, if a person is unable to pay for his services, he will render it without charge or else help to arrange such matters through some other source. You would do well to make prior arrangements with people in these areas, preferably among your own flock if such are available, to whom you may refer people who need their services.

In counseling you should learn to be a good listener. Sometimes a person simply wants to get something out of his system. Through the years I have had many people leave my office after such a session, saying how much better they felt, when I let them do most of the talking. Even when you need to give advice, you are not ready to do so until you know what is troubling someone. And, of course, any counsel you give should be of a spiritual nature and based upon the Bible. Where two people have a difference, such as husband and wife, it has been my experience that you never solve the problem unless both parties are present. When one or the other comes to you, hear him/her out. But eventually endeavor to get them together for joint counseling. At times people of other congregations will come to you simply because they do not want to talk to their pastor. In the case of unsaved people, your first effort should be to lead them to the Lord. As Jesus forgave the paralytic's sin before healing him, so you should seek to lead the unsaved to him who alone can forgive sin. If that is done, then you will have made a giant stride toward solving the acute problem. By the same token, inactive Christians should be led to identify with the church fellowship.

Many years ago in our city a prominent psychiatrist held a seminar for personnel directors of large businesses. He told them that each year thousands of people spend millions of dollars going to psychiatrists in search for something they could receive free in regular church attendance, but they do not know it is there.

The longer you stay in a pastorate, the greater will be the load of your counseling ministry. People must come to know and trust you. You can become a church's *preacher* by vote of the congregation. But you can become the people's pastor and counselor only as you earn the title. This is an argument in favor of long pastorates. I will even dare to say that you do not become a church's pastor in the deepest sense of the word until you have been there five years! This, of course, depends upon the size of the church. You do the best you can in shorter pastorates. But I am talking about the ideal. Through the years I was the *preacher* and *overseer* of many churches. I did my best to be their pastor. But I honestly feel that I was truly the pastor of only one church—the church where I remained for almost twenty-four years.

Once people come to know you and feel that they can trust you, they will tell you things about themselves that they will not reveal to any other person. I have often thought that if the walls of a pastor's office could talk, what stories of tragedy they would tell. But walls do not talk. *And neither should you!* Woe betide any pastor who betrays such a confidence! If you do, your ministry in that church is over. Suddenly your wife's health will call for a new climate. Confidential information should not be shared with either your wife or your secretary. It is better for their own sakes not to know some things. Certainly it is better for you and the conferee.

Most, if not all, states have laws which protect the confidential conversations of lawyers and physicians with clients/patients. Few, if any, provide such protection for pastors under similar circumstances. Often I have said, and meant it, that I would go to jail rather than to betray such a confidence from the witness stand in court. You should be willing to do the same.

Your service as the *bishop* or overseer in your church comes somewhat under the head of administrator. It involves plans, promotions, enlistment, and leadership in the detailed work of your church. Obviously, this task added to everything else is too much for you to do alone. So you will be wise to delegate responsibility. This relates to both your staff and your elected leadership. It also calls for organization of the work and the use of the organization. The average church has a tailor-made organization, including committee structure, which waits to be used. In case of a committee designed to care for a certain need, you should never bypass it but use it. The largest untapped resource of energy in a church is its lay leadership. The pastor who breaks down under a load of meticulous duties which could be handled by others, perhaps better than he can do it, shows his lack as an administrator. You are the *overseer,* not the lackey boy of everyone and everything!

As the overseer you are the chief administrator of the church program. Certainly you are the head of the staff. As we will see later (chap. 9) you should oversee their work, but do so through proper channels. Also, you are the overseer of the work of the elected leadership of the church. You are not their "boss," but you should supervise their work. But here also you should do so through channels. For instance, in the event you have a minister of education, you should work through him. Otherwise you should work through the director (superintendent) of the Sunday School and the corresponding officers of other organizations. You should maintain a warm relationship with these so that you become a co-laborer rather than a "boss." The same thing applies to your relations with the deacons and chairmen of church committees. You should never go over their heads in your supervision. They are there to be used, not to be ignored.

Naturally, for your supervision to be effective, you must be familiar with all phases of the work. Otherwise you will not know where to place your emphasis in leadership. It is better to provide inspiration for your workers than to use coercion. You should work closely with the church nominating committee to see that the best possible workers are procured. Then you should work with them, not at cross purposes with them. They should be inspired to work for the Lord and not merely for you. No pastor should ever build the church about himself. It should be built about the Lord. And you should so enlist and train a corps of workers so that should you leave the church, the work would not collapse but would go right on in your absence. Through use of a church cabinet, composed of leaders of organizations, you should build a team spirit working toward common goals.

Someone said that a shepherd's job is threefold: *fold* the sheep, *feed* the sheep, and *fleece* the sheep. All of these may be related to the duties of the *pastor.*

Folding the sheep is suggestive of reaching the lost for Christ and of enlisting Christians in the fellowship of service of the local church. However, this is only the beginning. Evangelism involves these things, but it also encompasses the development of those reached for Christ and his church. Feeding the sheep certainly involves your preaching and teaching ministry. But it also entails comfort in sorrow, care in sickness, rejoicing in happiness, and encouraging in times of trouble. You can get closer to your people in times of joy, such as the birth of a baby, and in times of sorrow than at any other time. In such cases they will respond more enthusiastically to attention and resent more deeply the lack of it. If at all possible, you should be the first one to visit the mother of a newborn baby and the first to call on those who have lost a loved one. Thus you bind your heart to their hearts with bonds of love which can never be broken. Through the years it has been my custom to write a letter to a new baby—not to the parents—in the hope that it will be the first letter the baby will receive. The response to this by the parents proves its effectiveness. They speak of placing these letters in baby books so that in later years the child may read his/her letter. Thus another bond is formed which proves helpful in ministering to that person's spiritual needs in the future.

You may preach *at* people on Sunday without being with them in their needs during the week, but without it you cannot preach *to* them. Such is time-consuming. That is all the more reason why in your office as bishop you should delegate certain responsibility to others. Furthermore, it will take its toll in emotional and spiritual strength. You cannot comfort people without first entering into their suffering. Neither can you rejoice with people in times of happiness unless you really share your joy with theirs. There will be times when you must go directly from the happy atmosphere of the birth of a baby into a home heavy with bereavement. And you must make the necessary adjustment between the two. Only the grace of God can enable you to do it and to sustain you in a never-ending change of circumstances. Thus you must constantly rely upon him who is the "chief Shepherd" (1 Pet. 5:4).

There is no higher calling than that of elder, bishop, and shepherd. And no other makes such demands. But the rewards exceed the effort. In my own experience there is no greater reward, humanly speaking, than to look back to the time when you performed the wedding ceremony for a couple, visited them when their first

baby was born, later led the child to Christ and baptized him/
her, eventually performing the wedding ceremony for the child
now having reached adulthood, and finally visited the new parents
when their child was born. It is thus that you fully know the
joy of being a pastor.

Extending Yourself

Earlier I have referred to the need of delegating responsibility.
It is thus that you extend your ministry through others. However,
before you can do this effectively you must enlist and train those
who will be your *other-self* in ministry. This calls to mind words
of the apostle Paul found in Ephesians 4:11–12. Referring to
Christ's ascension, he said, "And he gave some, apostles; and
some, prophets; and some, evangelists; and some, pastors and
teachers; for the perfecting of the saints, for the work of the ministry, for the edifying of the body of Christ." These he gave to
his people on earth.

The Greek text has no punctuation marks except a question
mark written like our semicolon. The translators punctuated as
they understood its meaning. The King James Version was translated by scholars of the Church of England where the *work* centered in the clergy. Thus this reads as if the labors mentioned
in verse 12 refer to the offices listed in verse 11. Therefore, we
are justified in removing the commas in verse 12. Doing so, for
instance, the role of "pastors and teachers" (one office) is for
the purpose of "perfecting [equipping] the saints [all Christians]
for the rendering of the ministry [serving] with the goal of building
up the body of Christ."

In this light it is evident that the pastor is not to do all the
work while others are merely spectators. The work of the Lord
is every Christian's responsibility. Church members cannot pay
others to do this work for them. To be sure, the laborer is worthy
of his hire (Luke 10:7). But paying that salary is not in any sense
the end of Christian obligation.

Thus the pastor is to extend his ministry by preparing others to do theirs. The word "perfecting" (Eph. 4:12) was used for equipping, such as a room with furniture. So the pastor is to equip others and develop them in the skills necessary for the proper use of their equipment. Perhaps we fail at this point more than at any other. We lead people to become babes in Christ. But we do not develop them into skilled adults in him. Such a process will require time, but it will be time well spent. General training should be given to all. But those possessing specialized skills should receive special attention to enable them to utilize those abilities in spiritual service. Any skill used in earning a legitimate living can also be used in serving the Lord.

Now this does not mean that as the pastor you can limit your service to training others. You must also lead by your example as you become involved in stated programs of activity. You cannot say, "Now I have trained you. You go and do it." Rather, you must say, "Come on! Let's go!" You are not only the equipper; you are the leader. As the shepherd goes before his sheep, so you must go before your people. No church will run ahead of its pastor. But filled with confidence through training, the people will respond to dedicated, enthusiastic leadership.

Difficult But Glorious

I would not be honest if I said that being a pastor is a bed of roses. It is not. In fact, I know of no more demanding position. You are never off the job. Prior to entering college my job required me to punch a clock. I thought how wonderful it would be to have work where this was unnecessary. But through the years as a pastor I have often thought how good it would be to have a job in which I could punch the clock at 5:00 P.M., go home, and know that I was not due back on the job until the next morning at 7:30. I should add, however, that it was only a fleeting thought.

While the pastor is always on the job, it is also true that in the broad picture he can set his own pace or schedule. And therein lies a danger. You can be the busiest person in town or the laziest.

You do not punch on or off the job. No one checks the mileage of your daily rounds. At the same time, however, your industry or lack of it will be evident in your degree of effectiveness in the pulpit and in the overall results of the church program. Your comparative freedom in your pace places an added burden upon you. Self-discipline is a *must.*

The difficulty is compounded in the fact that you are dealing with people. Unlike a mechanic, you cannot overhaul a human personality by replacing faulty parts. Unlike the physician, you cannot simply give someone a pill to ease his pain or operate to remove a sinful nature. Unlike a business executive, you cannot hire people and demand their cooperation. You are dealing with human personality, with souls, with the human will. Even God does not violate human personality or coerce the human will. Certainly you cannot do so. You can only inform, inspire, lead, and exhort.

To be the kind of pastor you should be calls for the wisdom of Solomon, the patience of Job, the vision of Isaiah, the courage of Amos, the love of Hosea, the strength of Samson, the leadership of Moses, the faith of Abraham, and the perseverance of Paul. This is a tall order. And you can live up to it only through dedication to God, love for people, the grace of the Lord, and total reliance upon the Holy Spirit.

However, there is also the glory. You serve the King of kings. You are a shepherd of souls and the bearer of good tidings to a confused, lost world. It was a great consolation to me when one day I realized that the Lord never told his servants to be successful, but to be faithful. You should do your best and leave the results with him. Thus at the end of the road you will hear the "well done" of him whose you are and whom you serve.

As I look back over the years of my ministry I can truthfully say that I would not exchange that role for any other. If I had ten thousand lives to live, I would want to spend every one of them as a pastor.

6

Preparation or Plagiarism?

Shortly after finishing the seminary, I was in the office of Dr. L. L. Gwaltney, editor of the *Alabama Baptist*. He was urging me to continue to study. A simple remark has remained with me through the years. "Some preachers are like wasps. They are bigger the day they are hatched than ever thereafter." He was impressing upon me that due to the demands for study in the seminary, such preachers know more at the time of their graduation than thereafter. Why? Because they cease to study. Someone said that preachers are put on the shelf five years after they put their books on the shelf. My only wonder about this statement now is whether he was generous in time.

So regardless of your many other duties, you should reserve time for study. Whether or not you do this will determine whether your preaching ministry will be characterized by *preparation* or by *plagiarism*.

Books of Sermons

One day I went to a Baptist Book Store and asked the manager for a scholarly book, a review of which I had read. Since she seldom had calls for such a book she said that she did not stock it, but would order it for me. Then she remarked, "One of the greatest disappointments I have in this work is to see the kind of books most preachers buy. For the most part they want books of sermons and nothing more."

Now there is nothing wrong with such books when they are properly used. Billy Graham and I were playing golf one day.

He had about two months between crusades. And he told me how he planned to use the time. In his library were shelves filled with books of sermons sent to him by publishers. In words something like these, he said, "I plan to read every one of these books simply to feed my own soul. If I am to be constantly giving out, I must also take in."

However, this is quite different from using such books as a crutch. You will find them useful as inspirational reading, as a source for new illustrations, and now and then for ideas which serve as sermon-starters. But beyond that it is a dangerous practice for you to become a slave to such—and worst of all to preach them as though they are your own. The proverbial two fingers held up as quotation marks at start and finish hardly satisfy the ethical matter involved.

Many years ago Dr. M. E. Dodd related this experience to me. He was in a county-seat town church for a revival. In the study with the young pastor just before the opening service, he said, "Now if you will tell me any problems you have in your church, I will try to deal with them in my sermons." The young pastor thanked him, but assured him he had no problems with which he could not cope. Then pulling a book of Dr. Dodd's sermons from a shelf, he said, "You feel free to preach on any subject you wish. But do not preach any of these sermons. If you do, my people will say that you are stealing my stuff."

Someone recently told me of an experience of Dr. Clovis Chappell, who in his time published many books of his sermons. He too was preaching in a revival and was using a series of messages from one of his books. About the middle of the week a man said to him, "Dr. Chappell, we are enjoying hearing you preach. But our people are disturbed because you are using our pastor's sermons." The next evening Dr. Chappell brought a volume of his book and showed it to the man.

It just happens that the late Dr. Herschel Ford and I have the same given name. He was noted for his "Simple Sermon" books. Through the years I have received many letters from preachers asking me to send them some of my "Simple Sermons." My reply is that all of my sermons are *simple*, but I am sure they are thinking about Herschel Ford.

For eighteen years I was the preacher on "The Baptist Hour." All of my sermons were printed by the Southern Baptist Radio and Television Commission and were made available by subscription. Often preachers tell me that they are preaching my sermons and that they hope I do not object. I laugh it off by saying, "Well, I tried to preach them, but couldn't; if you can preach them go right ahead." But deep in my mind I know that they are flirting with the danger of addiction to such, even if they are not already *hooked*.

I have related these instances to show the widespread practice of using a homiletical crutch. If you want to become a repetitious parrot of other men's sermons, that is your business. But if you want to develop a rich and more effective preaching ministry, you must pay the price of time, labor, and brain and soul sweat. It is only thus that with Paul you can speak of "my gospel." You alone can choose whether you will follow the road of *preparation* or *plagiarism*.

Building a Library

I will never forget the first time I entered the old library at Southern Baptist Theological Seminary. Over the entrance were these words: "Give Attendance to Reading (1 Timothy 4:13)." They made a lasting impression upon me.

In a very real sense, books are the tools of your trade. The Greek word for *reading* means to know again. The author knew it when he wrote the book. You know it again as you read it. Thus it is through the reading of books that you are able to look into the minds of the authors. Even so great a mind as that of Paul placed a great value on books. In his second letter to Timothy he said, "The cloak that I left at Troas with Carpus, when thou comest, bring with thee, and the books, but especially the parchments" (2 Tim. 4:13). He wanted his cloak to warm

his body, and his books and parchments to feed his mind and
soul. "Books" probably were papyrus rolls. "Parchments" renders
the word *membranas* (note "membrane"), probably more valuable
writings on dressed skins. These two items probably contained
copies of Old Testament books along with other writings. Even
while in prison, awaiting death, Paul did not neglect his study.
To him these things were like old friends. That he was well read
is evidenced in his quotations even from pagan writers (Acts 17:28;
Titus 1:12).

All of this suggests the importance of building your library.
It may contain many or few volumes. The important thing is
not their number but their quality. A wise investment for any
church would be to provide a fund for its pastor with which to
purchase books. Unfortunately, this is a rare thing. Nevertheless,
on your own you should purchase books—even if you have to
miss a few meals to do so.

Let us suppose that you are still in college or seminary. Your
textbooks could form the nucleus of your library. Unless it is
absolutely necessary to sell books from a course you have finished
in order to purchase those for a new course, you should not do
so. Discouraging such a practice, a seminary professor said that
when you sell such books you are disposing of the books about
which you know the most. Fortunately, I did not need to sell
my books. And through the years I have found them to be valuable
reference material.

As you build your library, of course the Bible itself should
occupy the central place. It would be well for you to have as
many translations of the Bible as possible. Thus you will find
many insights into the meaning of passages of Scripture under
study. For quick comparison you may want *The New Testament
from 26 Translations,* edited by Curtis Vaughan. I have found it
to be most valuable as a time saver.

If you are versed in the original languages, you should continue
to use your Hebrew Old Testament and Greek New Testament.
Only by continued use can you retain any degree of efficiency

in their use. So many of my contemporaries express regret that through the years they have not done so.

Every preacher's library should contain sets of good commentaries. *The Broadman Bible Commentary* gives you the benefit of scholarship with a minimum use of Hebrew and Greek words. While it is quite old, Dr. George W. Truett once said the *Matthew Henry's Commentary* was the best English commentary of which he knew. If you are versed in Hebrew and Greek *The International Critical Commentary* will prove helpful, as will A. T. Robertson's *Word Pictures in the New Testament* and *The Expositor's Greek Testament*. In addition to these standard works you may want single volumes on any of the books of the Bible. Any of the above may be found in religious book stores such as Baptist Book Stores.

I have found that an inexpensive way to add valuable helps to my library is the purchase of paperback study guide books published annually by Convention Press for the Bible Study Week sponsored by Southern Baptists. Usually certain other publishers provide their own books on the Bible book selected for this study. All of these are written by recognized scholars.

A good Bible dictionary and a Bible concordance should be a *must* in your library. In addition, you should have a Bible encyclopedia. For my need there is none better than the five-volume *The International Standard Bible Encyclopedia*. The last thing I did in preparing for my oral exam for my doctorate was to read every article in this set which dealt with the New Testament. It served as a refresher course covering the field of my study of two years. If you are a Southern Baptist you will want to include the three-volume set *Encyclopedia of Southern Baptists*. And speaking of such, why not secure some standard set such as the *Encyclopedia Britannica* as a reference work?

Included also should be books on theology; history, Christian and otherwise; poetry, especially religious poetry; science; biographies; *and a good dictionary*. In order to keep abreast in Christian thought you would do well to subscribe to religious periodicals such as *Review and Expositor, Southwestern Journal of Theology,* and *Christianity Today.*

But these are only the beginning. As you budget money to buy gasoline for your car to use in pastoral visitation, so you should budget money with which to purchase books. Add to your library carefully but regularly.

Let me suggest also that you not confine your purchase and reading of books to those with which you know you will agree. For one thing, you should know what is being written, if for no other reason than to be able to refute it in your preaching. Several years ago the "God is dead" movement caused quite a stir. In an address at the Southern Baptist Convention I paid my respects to it, including setting forth what it involved. Later a friend told me that someone sitting by him said, "You know, he has read the book." Does this mean that many were denouncing it without knowing what it meant? Reading such books will keep your mind sharp. You do not sharpen an axe by rubbing it with butter. You do so by use of abrasive material.

Provision for Study

Simply lining your library shelves with books does not make you a student. They are there to be used. The term "Pastor's study" is a reminder of this face. Your people expect you to use it for study.

In the usual situation your *study* will also be your *office.* And I fear that too often it is used for the latter more than for the former. For that reason it would be wise for you to have separate places for these functions. Most likely your office will be a part of an office complex. It is there that you will hold conferences and staff meetings, do counseling, and perform many other functions. Your study should be located in an out-of-the-way part of the church building. And its very decor should be conducive to study. For my part, in my study I prefer a large table instead of a desk. The table provides room for spreading out opened books. This is the working center.

For the purpose of general reading, a comfortable chair should be available. Such working tools as a typewriter on a portable table and/or other writing materials should be available according to your preference. Since I am not a skilled typist, I do all my writing in longhand. But I know others who just as effectively use a typewriter. It goes without saying that you should have at hand ample supplies of paper, paper clips, and other needed items.

Having your study separate from your office serves another very practical purpose. You will be spared the loss of time due to someone who just drops in to chat with the preacher. Furthermore, the staff will know that when you are in your *study* you are not to be disturbed except in cases of emergency.

Now having discussed the *usual,* let me present what I consider to be the ideal. That is to have your study in your home. However, this may not be the best arrangement when you have small children who do not understand that your study is off limits.

In our second pastorate out of the seminary the pastor's home had a study. But we also had an eighteen-month-old son. When I went into my study I closed the door. But as often happened, I was engrossed in study one day when the door opened. Our son toddled in carrying a Mother Goose book. I went right on studying, thinking that he might not disturb me. However, I soon felt him pulling on my leg. He crawled up in my lap, placed his book over my work, and said, "Daddy, weed." And you know what I did. Stopping my work, I "wead." However, as he grew older and could understand, having my study at home proved most helpful.

When I go to the church office I am in a business-administrative atmosphere. Should I try to study there, even behind closed doors, I hear typewriters going. Bits of conversation filter through the door. My mind is divided between studying and the thought that I need to see a staff member about something. Furthermore, should someone come by to see the pastor, I never wanted my secretary to tell a white lie by saying I was not in. The unpardonable sin to some people would be for her to say, "He is here. But he cannot be disturbed." However, if I were at home studying, she could honestly say that I was not in my office. And if there were some emergency she could always call me at home. Even at home, when I closed the door to my study it was an agreed signal with Mrs. Hobbs that I did not wish to be disturbed unless there was an emergency. She could screen phone calls. Many times the caller needed information which she could provide. Unless a matter needed immediate attention, she would take the phone number so that later I could return the call.

Also, having my study in my home enables me at times to study at night. Should I have nothing else to do and Mrs. Hobbs is busy at something, I can go into my study and spend a couple of hours. If my study were at the church I would not leave her at home alone. There is a difference between being across town and being down the hall. Furthermore, after making hospital calls or whatever, if I arrived home earlier than usual I could slip into my study for a few minutes or for an hour. A consulting psychologist in our church said that every person should budget forty-five minutes out of each hour, leaving fifteen minutes for the unanticipated. Mrs. Hobbs has accused me of budgeting one hour and fifteen minutes out of each hour. But remember that you can be the laziest or the busiest person in town. I prefer to be the latter. And so should you.

Program for Study

Now that you have a place in which to study and the tools for the same, you should use them. And during the time spent in your study you should *study*. To do so requires discipline and hard work.

For one thing, you should schedule a time for study, or other things will crowd in and monopolize the time. Administrative and pastoral duties are most demanding. It is possible for you to become so involved in them that you will neglect study habits which at the moment seem less pressing. It is precisely for this reason that you should set aside time dedicated to keeping your axe sharp. You may try to use the excuse that you do not have enough time for study. You have exactly the same amount of time as others do. It is not the amount of time you have but how you use it that matters. In a well-organized ministry you should make time for preparing your mind and spirit. In failing to do this, you shortchange both yourself and your people. Of course, you must strike a balance. As you should not constantly remain in an "ivory tower" away from the people, neither should you spend all of your time among them with scarcely any time left for study and preparation to preach to them.

It was reported that Dr. Truett waited until Saturday night after dinner to write out the outline of his sermons for the next day, sometimes on the back of an old envelope. Some preachers have sought to do this. But what they did not know about were the hours during the week that he spent in reading and other forms of study. He had so many books that the church had to build another room to his home to contain them. His study was just below his bedroom. It is said that many times in the wee hours of the morning Mrs. Truett would beat on the floor with a shoe to tell him to come to bed.

In most cases the best time to study is in the morning when your body and mind are fresh. I know of some preachers who go into their studies about 5:00 A.M. to work for a couple of hours before breakfast. The one danger I see in this is that you may deprive your body of needed rest—unless you retire early, something most of us do not do.

I have found that the best time for study is from 8:00 A.M. until just before noon. But as stated previously, I also study at other opportune times, especially at night. When I was a pastor I did much of my writing at night. In order to do this you should tell your people that, barring emergencies, you plan to study in the mornings, that you need to do this in order to be at your best in the pulpit. But assure them that you are available at any time in case of emergencies. You can request that otherwise they call the church office and you will return the call. It has been my experience that people will accept this in good grace—provided that they see the results in your pulpit ministry.

The first thing you should do when you enter your study each morning is to spend a quiet time with the Lord in Bible reading, meditation, and prayer. One of the greatest temptations for the preacher is to use the Bible only professionally. Before you can use it effectively as a tool of your trade, you must use it personally as through it God speaks to your heart. And since preaching is a sacred business, you should first seek the guidance of the Holy Spirit as you seek to comprehend the Bible's message. The Bible will not speak to others *through* you until first it has spoken from God *to* you. To paraphrase a beautiful little poem, you should commune with the Lord in the morning if you would have him through the day.

When you settle down to study, you should endeavor to free your mind from any other concern. Of course, the burdens of a pastor are always with him. But in any one phase of your ministry you must as far as possible let the others sink into your subconscious. This is especially true where study is concerned. Your mind can properly concentrate upon only one thing at a time. In this case it should be upon that which you are studying. And you can study properly only one thing at a time. It may be to read a good book. If so, then focus your full attention upon it. I find that it helps in this regard if I underline significant words, phrases, sentences, or paragraphs. This causes you to read more slowly and to think about the book's contents. Furthermore, when at some future time you return to a certain volume as a reference book, you can more readily identify the heart of its message on a given theme.

It may be that you are making an in-depth study of some particular doctrine. If so, you will certainly use your Bible and other books which deal with that doctrine. Do not come to this study with predetermined views except in regard to the basics. You will want to know what other writers think about it. But before accepting their views, be certain that they are in harmony with the Bible. Furthermore, as you study the Bible, do not talk to it but let it talk to you. Your responsibility is *exegesis,* drawing out that which is in the Scriptures—not *eisegesis,* reading into the Scriptures something that is not there.

It is helpful to read books about the Bible. But this should never become a substitute for studying the Bible itself. And remember that the criterion for interpreting the Bible is Jesus Christ. Beware of any interpretation of a passage of Scripture which is not in harmony with his life, person, teachings, and redemptive work! For he is the full and final revelation of God. God's written Word does not conflict with his living Word.

Concerning studying the Bible itself, it is profitable to study it by books. A suggested procedure would be to begin by determining the historical background of the book. Determine the environment which brought forth the book and the author's purpose in writing it. My old teacher A. T. Robertson followed the grammatico-historico method of interpretation. In other words, determine the historical setting and the meaning of the text itself. Thus the book will come alive with meaning. The historical setting will also enable you to apply its message in modern situations. "Introduction" sections of commentaries will prove helpful at this point. The same may be said of Bible encyclopedias.

There is an advantage in being familiar with the original language of a given book. But if this is not the case, at least you can study the many translations. Keep an English dictionary at hand in order to determine the exact meaning of unfamiliar English words. Where various meanings are possible, the Scripture context will enable you to choose the best one for your purpose.

When I propose to study a given book, after determining the historical setting I read through the book in more than one translation, without stopping, in order to follow the writer's thought. If you do not already know it, you will find a gradual unfolding of the author's purpose. Then, and not before then, you are ready to consult the body of commentaries in order to obtain the authors' understanding. If questions arise as you read the book, make notes of them; then deal with them in the closer commentary study. Final conclusions on the meaning of any passage should be your own as you feel led of the Holy Spirit. You may or may not find commentators who agree with you. Every translation and/or commentary reflects the author's own theological position. This is the reason why caution should be exercised as you weigh the product of their work.

But remember that the Bible sheds a lot of light on most commentaries. Furthermore, you should not plow around difficult verses or passages. Often when dealing with such I consult commentaries. I begin reading several verses before the difficult one. The writer will comment on easier verses, often telling me more than I want to know. But when he comes to the problem verse he will make some meaningless comment and then move on. I simply smile and say, "He does not know its meaning either." However, this should not lead you to ignore the verse or passage. Stay with it until you at least have learned something about it. It may be that you are the one to whom the Holy Spirit will give added insight into it.

In 1977 Dr. R. G. Lee had a heart attack while in Oklahoma City. When I visited him in the hospital he said, "Now, Beloved, after we have had prayer I want you to do something for me." Later he said that the only verse in the Bible he did not understand was 1 Corinthians 11:10. He wanted me to write out my interpretation of it and give it to him, which I did. But the point is that at ninety years of age he was still trying to grub out a *stump*.

It has been my rare but happy privilege to have some New Testament professor thank me for a fresh insight into a passage of Scripture—one which he had not seen. I have told them that even a blind hog will find an acorn every once in awhile. The *acorns* are there. And you may be the person to find some of them. One day I received a letter from Dr. W. W. Adams, professor of New Testament at Southern Baptist Theological Seminary. He commented favorably on a book I had written on Colossians. Then he made this significant statement. "You pastors see things in the Bible that we professors often do not see." The reason is that they are primarily concerned about technical matters. We pastors are asking what a passage says to our people. We are looking for something to preach.

I was in A. T. Robertson's class on a Monday afternoon in 1934, when a stroke was coming on him which caused his death less than two hours later. On Friday before he died, he paid what probably was his greatest compliment to the Bible. After noting that for more than fifty years he had been studying, teaching, preaching, and writing about the New Testament, he said, "I never open my Greek New Testament but that I find something in it that I have not seen before."

A young man entered the ministry and a year later announced that he was leaving it. His reason was, said he, "I have run out of anything to preach!" If you stick to your Bible you will never run out of something to preach. Rather, you will want to live a thousand years so that you can preach its glorious message.

And do not be disturbed about adverse critics of the Bible. I am told that rabbits tend to run in circles. If you wait long enough it will come back to the area from which it started. I would not know about that. But one thing I do know. I have lived long enough to see hundreds of once-disputed questions about the Bible vindicated by archaeology and other sciences. In my judgment, where such passages still exist the problem is not with the Bible but with man's understanding. Scholars will still chase their *rabbits*. But take your stand with the Bible; and when the rabbit has run its course—when ample information on a problem passage is available—the *rabbit* will come and lie down at your feet.

Now let me share with you one of my experiences in Bible study which has proved most beneficial to me. Years ago in a New Testament class in the seminary Dr. W. Hersey Davis challenged us to take familiar passages of Scripture which over the years have been plowed and harrowed near the surface, resulting in interpretations that are commonly known to those who hear preaching with regularity. Then set your plow so as to go deeper and turn up fresh soil or meanings. Such a method will result in fresh interest in Scripture and preaching. Whether or not I have succeeded, I have tried to do this through the years.

For instance, when I was asked to write a book on the seven sayings of Jesus from the cross, I read every book I could find in this field. My discovery was that with one exception the authors had said the same thing, only using different words to say it. The thought occurred to me to study these sayings from the standpoint of the papyruses, current documents, and writings of the general time of Jesus. What did these sayings mean to Jesus' contemporaries who for the first time heard them in a Christian context? Using Moulton and Milligan's *The Vocabulary of the Greek New Testament* as the base, I uncovered a mother lode of truth. Applying the results of this study, these sayings came alive with fresh meaning I had never seen before. I have since followed the same procedure with other New Testament books, which produced similar results.

Some years ago an extremely wealthy man died in Houston, Texas. He made his fortune by obtaining drilling rights from large oil companies which had abandoned former oil fields, thinking that they had pumped them dry. This man drilled deeper and found larger pools of oil than the original ones nearer to the surface. I understand that many oil companies now follow this method with highly rewarding results.

This same method can be applied to the Bible. There is "gold in them thar hills" or in oil fields, if you please. The deeper message of the Bible is inexhaustible. So why should you be content to continue scratching the surface of a worked-out level of truth? The Scriptures have much to say to us which has not yet been said, if we are willing to pay the price.

This suggests another matter. Often I have been asked how, as a busy pastor and denominational worker, I have found time to write so many books. The answer is manifold: I have an understanding wife who lets me spend the necessary time; I have my study in my home; I work by a schedule; I have had an understanding church which permitted me to study; and I have had a staff which helped me bear other loads in order to free me for this work. But in addition to all these, writing is my principal method of study.

My mind will be as lazy as I will let it be. If I am simply preparing a sermon for next Sunday, I will be tempted to gather just enough material for that sermon. And the result may be a serving of soup instead of a strong, balanced meal. A man once said to me that most of the sermons he heard were like soup. They had a little bit of everything but not much of anything in them. It did not take him long to get enough of it. But it did not stay with him very long after he had eaten/heard it. You should not be content to keep your people on a soup diet when what they need is strong meat. A diet of soup produces weak Christians. Strong meat is necessary if they are to grow up in him and render effective service for him. Paul complained that he had to feed the Corinthian Christians on milk rather than meat because they were weak babies—carnal or flesh-controlled Christians (1 Cor. 3:1–2). He had to do this of necessity, even as we may need to do with young Christians. But we should not deprive those who prefer a juicy steak over a bowl of soup. You should learn a lesson from those who plan a menu. Begin with soup, but then move on to more nourishing food.

The reason that I have majored on writing as a means of study stems from this very thing. If I am going to write something I hope will be published in book form, I am challenged to do my best to write something that will merit being published. Having done this with a given book of the Bible, when later I come to preach on some portion of it, my spade work has already been done. Then it is largely a matter of selecting what to use in keeping with my purpose, arranging it in orderly form, and determining what applications to make of it for the needs of my listeners.

Preparing to Preach

The demands for two messages on each Sunday and one on Wednesday night are great. This means that in the course of a year you must prepare 156 messages—to say nothing of other demands for speaking. If you view it as a whole, you may be tempted to cry, "Who is sufficient for these things?" No one is, except in the power of the Holy Spirit. However, you should look at these messages one at a time and plan ahead so as to be equal to the task.

One day at the seminary a group of us talked about what method each used in preparing sermons in addition to a heavy load of study. Different ones set forth different approaches. Finally one man spoke whose words reeked with an air of superiority. "I do not use any of these methods. Many times I go into the pulpit not knowing what I am going to say." I hope it was the Lord and not the devil who prompted my response. But calling him by name, I said, "Yes, and I imagine that many times you come out of the pulpit not knowing what you have said." Someone asked another what his pastor preached about on the previous Sunday. He replied truthfully, "He never did say." Shame on us if that can ever be said of our preaching!

Now successful sermon preparation calls for careful planning. Preachers have been known to use as an excuse for not studying that the Holy Spirit will fill their mouths. This is to misinterpret Matthew 10:18–20. If you would claim this promise you should be brought into court while being persecuted for your faith. Dr. Davis related this promise to the time before the writing of the New Testament. To use this promise of Jesus as an excuse for not studying is not piety but *pure laziness!* As a boy on a farm it was my job periodically to take corn to the grist mill to have it ground into meal. It was evident that unless the miller put corn in at the top, no meal came out at the bottom. The machinery ran furiously with much noise. But it yielded no meal. And the same principle applies to you as a preacher. You must put wisdom and knowledge in your brain if you want *meal* to flow from your mouth. Otherwise, in the pulpit you will be nothing more than furious effort and noise. Your mouth will be filled, to be sure— but not by the Holy Spirit. It will be filled with wind and noise.

You should plan ahead for your preaching program. What are the needs of your people? What doctrines should you emphasize?

What programs will you want to deal with from the pulpit? I would suggest that you should plan your preaching program generally at least one year ahead. Certain stated seasons and events provide you with a ready-made guide for much of this preparation: Easter, Mother's Day, Father's Day, Thanksgiving, revival preparation, budget campaigns, and the like. The program should be specifically laid out six months in advance. For three months before preaching a given sermon, you should give to it increasing attention as the time approaches for its use. Why not use an *assembly line* method. Place the sermons in the order they will come. In your general observations and reading, ideas will come which can be filed with a given sermon. Actual preparation for a sermon should begin not later than two weeks before you preach it.

Let me slip this thought in at this point. Through the years I have made a study of "Orders of Worship." Usually they show careful preparation as anthems and hymns are listed by name, number in the hymnal, and the author. But when I come to what should be the climax of the service I read "Sermon: Message by the Pastor." No sermon title and Scripture reference are given. This says to me that as late as early in the previous week when the bulletin went to press, the pastor did not know what he would use for his sermon the following Sunday. Maybe he knew. But the absence of a sermon topic leaves the opposite impression. Such should not be the case.

Having done your research, place appropriate ideas in an orderly fashion so as to produce a climax at the close of the message. Illustrations should be selected which will aid in clarifying your thoughts. Everyone will use his own method of filing such for future use. I find that illustrations from life *live* far better than those gleaned from a book of such. You can train your mind to do what you wish. In this regard, illustrations from observing and living life I file in my subconscious. As I pore over a portion of a sermon, the proper illustration seems to rise into my consciousness. Doing so, it *lives*.

Is this a haphazard method? For some, it may be. But the

following example shows that it is practical for me. Some years ago a seminary student wrote his master's degree thesis on my "Baptist Hour" preaching. Among other things he noted this method and raised the question about repetition of the same illustrations. Then he made the following comment. Out of several hundred of my sermons he examined, I had not used the same illustration twice. This may not be your way of doing it. But have a way suited to your disposition. Do not leave it to chance!

I have heard the charge made that long-range planning rules out the leadership of the Holy Spirit. I say that the opposite is true. He can guide you far better in a quiet, orderly, and pressure-free situation than he can in a case of panic on your part or Saturday night between dinner and bedtime. I am certain that all of us have had the experience of coming to that time with no idea about what we will preach the next day. Frantically we turn the pages of the Bible. But there does not seem to be a sermon in it. On the other hand, when you read your Bible calmly and devotionally, sermon ideas leap from its pages like trout in a lake. It is true that some of your best ideas will at times come from the Holy Spirit as you preach. But this is because to the best of your ability you have done your part. Conversely, when I have not prepared properly before preaching, some of my best ideas for a given sermon came to me on the way home *after* I have preached it. The Holy Spirit does not work by magic. Rather, he works through dedicated preachers who expend brain and soul sweat in preparing to preach.

Once you have gotten a hold on your sermon, you must let it get a hold on you. This will come as you familiarize yourself with its contents, pray through it as you agonize in your soul, and preach it to yourself in your mind and heart. It is then, and only then, that you are ready to preach.

7

Prophet or Performer?

Preaching is serious business. When Paul spoke about "the foolishness of preaching" (1 Cor. 1:21) he was not speaking of the act of preaching but of "the thing preached" or the message. To unsaved Jews and Gentiles the message of a crucified Savior was respectively a stumbling block and foolishness or moronic. But those who believed in him found that in this message was both the power and wisdom of God for salvation.

For this reason you should never take lightly this phase of your ministry. You are a *prophet* sent from God to a given occasion and people. Certainly, then, you should be a prophet and not a mere performer. Indeed, if you are the latter you may well be called a false prophet. Any attitude, conduct, or message which belittles the office is truant to this calling and duty.

Assuming that you have lived with your people during the week, you are aware of their joys, sorrows, problems, and needs. Furthermore, you have spent time alone with the Lord as you have prepared in mind, heart, and spirit to proclaim his message. In a very real sense the hours of worship and proclamation on the Lord's day are the climax to the entire week. Therefore, you should seek to make the most of them. As God's called man, you should endeavor to lead the people in a true experience with God through worship and preaching from his Word. And as you have prepared yourself beforehand to preach, so you should have done both to worship and to lead your people in worship. In this sense you will fill the dual role of priest and prophet. But we will deal with it under the general term of *prophet*.

Prophet Defined

What is a prophet, anyway? So often when the word is used people think of someone who foretells the future. This was one role of a prophet in both the Old and New Testaments. It is clearly seen in the Old Testament prophets. To a lesser degree it is found in the New Testament (Acts 11:27–28).

The Greek verb for the act of prophesying is *propheō*. It means both to speak before and to speak forth, or to foretell and to tell forth. While the Old Testament prophets did at times foretell the future, the greater burden of their prophecies was to tell forth God's message to their own generations. This latter ministry is even more pronounced in the New Testament. In this sense a Christian prophet is one who preaches the gospel with power. So knowing the serious nature of your prophetic office, you should approach it in humility, earnestness, and total reliance upon God. You should not see your role as simply an honor. But you should honor it by the manner in which you fill it.

Debasing the Office

The other side of the coin is that you should avoid any attitude or conduct in the pulpit which tends to debase your role as a prophet. People have a high regard for one who speaks for God. But their regard for your role will be in direct proportion to your own regard for it. Therefore, for a few minutes let us consider the matter of pulpit manners.

For instance, take the simple matter of pulpit dress. In those groups which major on ritual, the pastor often wears a pulpit gown. But among those who place a greater emphasis upon preaching, this hardly seems appropriate. It helps to perpetuate the false idea of separation between clergy and laity. "Mod" suits may be the "in thing" among young people. But to wear such in the pulpit detracts from the prophetic office.

In my judgment, in the pulpit you should be dressed modestly and neatly. A dark gray, blue, or black business suit with shoes, shirt, and tie to match seem to be best for the occasion. Jewelry should be kept to a minimum. It may sound rather *picky,* but you should wear knee-length socks so that no part of your legs will show. Any oddity about your appearance will serve to distract the congregation. You want to blend into the congregation so that you become a part of them. Your desire is that the people will concentrate on the Lord and not on you.

Of even greater importance is your conduct. A simple rule to follow is that what is wrong for all the people to do during a worship service is wrong for you to do. For instance, you should avoid whispering to the one seated by you on the platform. If some vital matter must be communicated, it should be done as briefly and inconspicuously as possible. However, such cases should be absolutely necessary and as rare as possible. A brief note will serve the purpose without being noticed.

Furthermore, your posture will communicate your attitude to the people. For this reason you should not slump down in your chair or cross your legs as if to get comfortable for what you consider an ordeal before you. Both feet should be planted squarely on the floor; you should sit erect, perhaps leaning slightly forward as if in eager anticipation. You should focus your attention on what is being said and done by others. Even the expression on your face should be one of alert but quiet serenity. When the congregation sings you should sing. This shows that you are a participant in and not merely an observer of the worship service. If you do not sing, just suppose that the congregation followed your example. It would result in dead silence other than the instrument while the music leader just swung his arms for the exercise.

When someone else leads in prayer, you should bow your head and pray. If you decide to sneak a peep at the congregation, you may be certain that some of them are doing the same. And they will know that you are not praying. Spiritual forces are so delicate and sensitive that these irreverent atttiudes will affect adversely the tone of the entire service. When the choir or a soloist sings just before the sermon, it will be well for you to bow your head, close your eyes, and meditate and pray.

I suppose that it is my devilish spirit, but I get a kick out of reminding W. A. Criswell of an incident which took place in a worship service many years ago. His daughter Mabel Anne (Anne Criswell Jackson) was very young. Through the years he has done as suggested above just prior to the sermon. One Sunday Mabel Anne asked her mother what he was doing. Betty whispered, "Daddy is praying that God will give him a good sermon." The little tyke replied, "Well, why doesn't God ever do it?" Of course, God always did/does. But she was too young to appreciate it.

Now these are but a few commonsense suggestions. Perhaps you will think of others. But by all means do not observe them as mere mechanical, play-acting things. (Incidentally, the Greek word rendered "hypocrite" means a play-actor.) They should be done as a genuine effort to become one with a worshiping congregation. If done in this spirit, they will enhance the whole of your pulpit ministry.

Be Yourself!

In this section I want to point out some dangers which you should avoid with respect to your pulpit ministry. In one way or another they relate to things in which, to say the least, you will come out second best even if you succeed. For at best you will only be a fair imitation of the real thing.

Someone said that the present generation is one which has no heroes. If true, it is a sad thing. But I suspect that this is more cynicism than realism. Quite often you read about some athlete who points to an older one, saying, "He has always been my hero." By this he means that he looks up to him in admiration and aspires to be as good an athlete as he was/is. I am certain that this is true today among preachers. I know that it was the case with my generation. Perhaps you have selected some older preacher who has been successful in his preaching. You want to succeed in yours. Thus you select him as your model. If so, it speaks well of both you and him.

But there is a subtle danger to be avoided. So often we equate one's greatness with his peculiarities or those things which set him apart from others. For instance, I am thinking about a music teacher who for many years taught in a seminary school of music. He has long since gone to be with the Lord. And due to the passage of time, most of his students have done the same or else have retired from regular positions. But so long as they were around I could usually spot those whose hero he had been—not necessarily by their achievements, equal to his in church music, but by one thing which stood out above all others.

As a young man this teacher had worked in a sawmill. In an accident he had lost the first two joints on the middle fingers on his right hand. Thus, when he directed music, he did so with the thumb and the first and little fingers on his right hand, with two stubs in between. Yes, you guessed it. Many of his former students with whole right hands did the same thing by bending downward the second and third fingers on that hand. Perhaps they did so unconsciously. But to those who knew the relationship, it was evident as to the source of this practice.

Some preachers do the same thing. Dr. John A. Broadus was one of the four professors who were the founders and first teachers at Southern Baptist Theological Seminary. He later was also its president. In addition to being a prominent scholar he was also a great preacher. But he also had a slight physical defect—he was hump-shouldered. I am told that many young preachers wanted to be a great preacher like Dr. Broadus. But they did not master the Greek New Testament as he did or become the great homiletician he was. Instead, I am told that they went about the campus with their perfectly straight shoulders humped over!

Dr. L. R. Scarborough, president of Southern Baptist Theological Seminary, was a prominent teacher of evangelism and an excellent preacher. But he had the habit when preaching of pulling down on the lobe of, I believe, his left ear. Many of his students wanted to be a great preacher like Dr. Scarborough. As a result, it was said that many of his former students had longer lobes on their left ears!

In a poll to select the greatest single preacher in Southern Baptist history, doubtless George W. Truett would win by a landslide. I have said many times that he is the nearest one to being a canonized saint that Southern Baptists have ever had. Behind his back we lovingly called him "Marse George." Quite naturally he was the ideal of most young preachers of that era.

When he stood to preach you could almost hear a pin drop after he had captured his listeners by sweeping the crowd with his eagle eyes. His style in preaching was to begin low and slow, then to increase in volume and tempo as he reached climax after climax, finally carrying his audience right up to the throne of grace.

In his voice was a note of pathos unlike any other I ever heard. It was born of a great sorrow and tragedy. In his earlier years as pastor in Dallas, he and a deacon went deer hunting. As is customary, they separated for the hunt. Seeing a movement among some trees and thinking it was a deer, Dr. Truett shot. Soon he learned that he had unknowingly killed his deacon. Naturally he was plunged into the deepest depths of grief and sorrow. In that condition he vowed never to enter the pulpit again. His people insisted that he do so. On the following Sunday as he began to preach, the people heard a note of pathos which had never before been present. It was born of a broken heart! And it stayed with him the rest of his days. Perhaps this note added to his other abilities made him the superb preacher that he was.

Quite naturally younger preachers wanted to become great preachers like Dr. Truett. So for many he became the model after which to pattern. In doing so, they sought to imitate him. I can honestly say that the only thing I tried to achieve from him was his clear enunciation. To whatever degree I have succeeded I am glad. But many sought to imitate his note of pathos. But what was so effective in him was far from such in those who had endured no such sorrow as his. To those who knew the situation, such cheap imitations were positively disgusting!

I quote from a biography of Dr. Truett by his son-in-law, Powhatan W. James.

"Some time ago another preacher who, rightly or wrongly, is accused of essaying the Truett manner of speech was addressing the Southern Baptist Convention on a subject in which the messengers were greatly interested. This brother prolonged his low tones too long. None save those on the front seats could hear what he was saying. Finally, a messenger far away in the gallery stood up and shouted: 'Louder! Louder! We can't hear a word you say.' Whereupon a big-voiced messenger near the front boomed out at the gallerite: 'Well, thank God, and sit down.'"

Several years ago I read a book by Dr. Roy McClain. In it he related an experience which is common to every young preacher. Contemplating his own ministry, he asked himself after which great preacher he should pattern his preaching. As mentally he ran through a list of noted pastors, a thought struck him. Should he choose any one of these, he might or might not live up to his pattern. Even if he did, he would only be a copy of someone else. Then he asked himself who was the only unique person he knew. Obviously the answer was himself. So he determined "to be the best me I could be." He would be himself to the best of his ability. This would be a good decision for you to make.

Amateurs Among Professionals

Another temptation which besets every preacher is to try to be something he is not. When he does he ceases to be a prophet and becomes a performer.

Take, for instance, the field of entertainment—specifically that of humor. There are some preachers who have a natural sense of humor, and others who have none at all. Some of the latter have been successful in developing one. It is a blessed moment when a preacher learns to face life with a smile, and even to laugh with others about himself without embarrassment. I have often said that if I did not have a sense of humor I would be miserable—and, perhaps, dead long ago.

However, I am thinking at present about the preacher who

seeks to be a humorist at the expense of his preaching. You should never seek to become a pulpit Bob Hope or Jack Benny or to think that the people have come together to see you perform. They have come to hear you preach God's Word. They are not primarily interested in what you have learned from a joke book or a column in a publication. They want to know what you have learned from God's book, not to hear the latest joke you have heard. They want to know what you have heard from the Lord. And just remember, when you seek to be a humorist rather than a herald, you are an amateur trying to compete with professionals. Thus you cheapen yourself, your position, and the message you are sent to declare.

This is not to say that good, wholesome humor has no place in your ministry. The story is told of a Christian woman who associated piety with a long face and who tried to win another to Christ. In her saddest tone and with her most miserable countenance, she asked, "Do you want to be a Christian?" The other lady replied, "No. I am miserable enough as it is."

Jesus had a sense of humor. Can you imagine him being so popular on the banquet circuit had he been a wet blanket? A careful reading of his teachings reveals this humor. The figure of a man with a log sticking out of his eye while trying to remove a speck of dust from another's eye is humor at its best. Elton Trueblood wrote a book on the humor of Jesus. I regret that he beat me to it.

Somewhere the idea got started that Dr. Truett had no sense of humor. I never heard him tell a joke, though I am told that he did at times in personal groups. I once saw him sit on a platform and laugh heartily at jokes told by Dr. Merton Rice, a Methodist preacher—and at his own expense no less. Someone told me that when he was in a revival, with his associate Bob Coleman leading the singing, in his room after services he had Coleman tell him jokes to relax. At times he would say, "Now, Bob, tell me the one about . . ." referring to one he had already heard and liked especially.

There is a time and place for good things, a time to weep and a time to laugh. With a supply of good humor you can brighten a social occasion, provided you do not try to monopolize the situation. Tense moments in a church or denominational business meeting may be eased by your telling an appropriate joke. When you are introduced to speak on an occasion, religious or otherwise, a good funny story will help you to form a rapport with your audience. At times an appropriate joke can even serve to introduce a sermon. Such may also serve to illustrate points in a sermon. If you sense that your listeners are restless or if the sermon is unduly long, an appropriate joke will relax them and regain their attention.

What you should avoid is telling one joke after another when you should start to preach. The people are there not to be entertained, but to be instructed in spiritual matters, inspired, encouraged, comforted, aroused to action for the Lord, convicted of sin, and led to trust Jesus as Savior. Certainly you may use humor, but do so wisely.

Another thing to avoid in the pulpit is to speak authoritatively and dogmatically in areas in which you are not qualified to do so. For instance, I am thinking of fields such as law, medicine, economics, sociology, and the various sciences.

The following story illustrates the point. A young unmarried preacher had heard the usual mother-in-law jokes. So on Mother's Day he proceeded to consign them to the nethermost regions. His own mother was present. After the service when they were alone, she asked, "Did it ever occur to you that I am a mother-in-law?" Nuf sed!

To borrow a phrase from Dr. Robert G. Lee, in strange areas you should not walk with the presumptuous step of a know-it-all. For again you are an amateur in the field of professionals. Your people generally will be aware of your lack of qualification, so to speak. And one of these professionals may be present. He/she may be the very person you want to reach. Instead, you will more likely lose him. This person, knowing that you know so little about his field, will question whether you know anything about the spiritual matters of which you speak.

I am not saying that you should not deal with such areas in your preaching. You should, for, after all, they are a part of the broad spectrum of life. They may furnish a rich source of illustrations and examples in putting across the major theme of your message. When you do use them, however, you should be certain as to your facts. Why not check them out with someone who is qualified to speak in a given area? It goes without saying that you should not use *lectures* on any of the above-mentioned fields as substitutes for *sermons* taken from the Bible. Current events may be used to introduce sermons and to illustrate their contents. But commentaries on such have no place in the pulpit. Your people can keep up with these as presented by experts through newspapers and the electronic media.

I once knew a prominent pastor who went to Europe when such a trip was rare. He visited the leading art galleries of Europe. Upon his return home he announced a three-month series of Sunday night lectures on great masterpieces of art. It was a question as to which would end first—his series or his Sunday evening services. A lady who loved her former pastor very much told me she once asked him when he was going to stop preaching from the *Reader's Digest* and start preaching from the Bible. Ouch! No one should ever need to ask you such a question.

No one person can be a master in all fields of life. Most of us do well to attain a fair degree of competency in one. If there is any one area in which you should be able to speak with any degree of authority, it is the Bible. In all likelihood, when you stand in your pulpit and preach the Bible, you will know more about it than any other person present. But if this be not the case, even the selective few also need to hear preaching. A massive mind will have a hungry soul as much as the most unlearned in the congregation. And when you preach, do not aim your message at the scholars. Preach so that all may hear and be fed. It is still true that if you put the feed down where the calves can reach it, you need have no fear about the cows getting their share.

You will notice that I said to *preach the Bible,* not preach from it. Not too long before he died the late Dr. Raymond Brown, distinguished professor of New Testament at Southeastern Baptist Theological Seminary, said to me, "Many preachers call themselves Bible preachers because they preach from the Bible. But a Bible preacher preaches the Bible." This suggests the importance and value of expository preaching, the best form of preaching. It is also the most demanding form of preaching for the preacher. As the word *expository* suggests, it is to draw from the Bible what it says and then apply it to the lives of your listeners.

The Bible is a logical book. Thus you will find in it a built-in outline. However, it demands depth in study to ascertain its message and how it speaks to our present needs. But if you are willing to pay the price, you will find that expository preaching yields many values. For example, it centers your message in God's word. Thus you can truly say, "Thus saith the Lord." It enables you to avoid doctrinal hobbies. It furnishes a balanced diet for your people. You will never lack for something to preach. It will instruct your people in biblical truth as it speaks to their needs. If you stick to the Bible instead of simply voicing your own opinions, you have a perfect answer for criticism of your preaching. If you step on someone's toes and he complains, you can say, "Well don't get mad at me. Take it up with the Lord. I simply told you what he says in his Word." Long pastorates for the most part are built on expository preaching. And even if you desire to move up in the scale, to be known as a Bible preacher will make you more attractive to pulpit committees. People want to hear Bible preaching.

I am a football *nut.* A team may have a few razzle-dazzle plays. But when it is hard put to it in a game, it always returns to basics in its repertoire of plays. God's *team* is finding the going tough as it faces an age such as ours. It is high time that we returned to the basics—preaching the Bible. You should do so faithfully. And leave the results with him whose word it is. He has promised that his word will not return unto him void (Isa. 55:11).

Some Positive Suggestions

Before concluding this chapter I want us to return to the idea of conduct in the worship service in order to point out some positive matters for you as the pastor. In the portion of the service where you are the direct leader, you should strive to be at your best. I am thinking of Scripture reading, prayer, sermon, and invitation.

You will notice that I did not list *announcements* and *welcome to visitors*. These can be handled by someone else. Since announcements are printed in the order of worship, there is no need to repeat them vocally. Periodically the people might be reminded that due to lack of space, only those events of primary importance and general interest are printed in the program. As the pastor you can add your emphasis to the welcome for visitors just prior to the benediction. This will also serve as a reminder to the members to greet the visitors personally after the service.

The time set apart for the reading of the Scripture and the pastoral prayer is a solemn one. It should be used in keeping with its nature. Therefore, you should plan as carefully for these as you do for your sermon. I have heard some preachers read a selected passage of Scripture as if they were seeing it for the first time and lead the pastoral prayer as if caught by surprise and not knowing what to say except to mouth the usual phrases. These sacred moments deserve better treatment than this.

Though it may not always be the case, the Scripture to be used usually will be determined by the sermon text. This is especially true in expository preaching. Even if another passage should be used, it should complement the text and the sermon. Whatever passage is used, it should be printed in the order of worship. This will not only suggest careful planning; it also will enable those with Bibles to turn to the passage beforehand.

It is evident, therefore, that preparation for reading the Scripture begins long before Sunday morning. After finishing your sermon for a given service, you should spend time studying the selected passage. If it is the one from which you plan to preach, you will already be aware of its detailed meaning. Now you must familiarize yourself with it as a whole. Seek afresh to recreate in your mind the actual event depicted. Enter psychologically into the experiences of any characters involved. Study the punctuation. Determine where you should pause, where you should slow or increase the tempo, where you should raise or lower your voice, and which words to stress. Then you should read it aloud over and over again until it becomes second nature to observe these elements effectively. Like an athlete practicing a play, do this until you can read the passage instinctively. It would be well before going into the pulpit on Sunday to refresh yourself by reading it afresh.

When you stand to read the Scripture in the service, you should endeavor to be relaxed. You should by this time be so familiar with the passage that you can either read it from memory or else with only an occasional glance at the page. Thus you can establish and maintain eye contact with the people. Read the passage naturally, using your ordinary tone of voice. Visualize the scene and place yourself in it. Because of your previous preparation you should be able to read with the proper cadence, voice inflection, and clear enunciation. If you make the scene live for you, you can be certain that it will live for those who hear you. Both you and the people will be prepared for the sermon soon to follow.

I will always be grateful to "Prof" Johnson of Southern Seminary for his patience and effort in teaching me and others how to read the Scriptures. He not only made it effective but enjoyable. For instance, he used selected passages designed to reveal our common faults and how to correct them. One such passage was 1 Thessalonians 4:13. He would have one of us to stand before the class and read. Usually the student would keep his eyes glued to the page and read slavishly in a monotone with no thought of punctuation or inflection. The result would be something like

this, "I would not have you ignorant brethren." At that point
he would break in, saying, "Do you know how you read it? Listen.
'I would not have you ignorant brethren on a Christmas tree.'"
After the laughter subsided, he would demonstrate the proper
way to read it. It is difficult to reproduce it in cold print. But
let us give it a try, using italics to show voice inflections. "I would
not have you *ig*norant, *breth*ren, concerning them which are
asleep." I suggest that you try reading it both ways to see the
difference in beauty of expression and meaning. By applying these
simple rules, you can make the reading of Scripture a delightful
and meaningful experience.

Much of the same thing applies to the preparation for leading
in the pastoral prayer. Certainly this should not be an afterthought
or something left to chance. You should never pray off the top
of your head, so to speak, or simply utter whatever words which
happen to come to mind. Leading a congregation to the throne
of grace is no simple matter and should never be done haphazardly.
Peter Marshall is remembered more for his prayers than for his
sermons.

As you prepare to read and preach, so you should prepare to
pray. In a quiet time during the week you should pray, "Lord,
teach us [me] to pray" (Luke 11:1). And "teach" on the Lord's
part implies *study* on your part. Ask yourself questions. What
are my needs and those of the people? Who in my knowledge
needs prayer now in given situations: sorrow, problems, troubles,
temptations, and joys? Endeavor to visualize these people so that
they become persons, not blobs. What is there in the church program or the denomination which should be included? These are
but sample questions. You may think of others in your given
situation. As you come to pray, your prayer will not just be a
blanket to throw over the world. While you do not need to call
names, you can visualize people and specific needs. And as you
do this, rest assured that those whom you lead will mentally add
their list to yours.

Once you have determined the contents of your prayer, you

may want to write it out—not for the purpose of reading it from the pulpit, but of giving a proportionate body to your prayer. The prayer should contain the proper elements. It should be directed to Deity and should contain worship, praise, thanksgiving, petition, confession, plea for forgiveness, and dedication—in that order. And it should be prayed in Jesus' name, through his merit and by his authority.

Caution should be observed as to the manner in which you address God. For instance, to address him as the "great God of the universe" tends to make him seem to be so far away. We can do no better than to follow Jesus' example when he said, "Our Father." While you should pray to God as near at hand, you should avoid overfamiliarity. You should not talk to him as you would to a *buddy*. He is the exalted Father who is ever near but also exalted. He is both immanent and transcendent.

Should you be invited to Buckingham Palace, you would not greet the queen by saying, "Hi, Liz!" Or in the White House you would not say, "Hi Jimmy, old boy!" You would say "Your Majesty" or "Mr. President." If you address human leaders with respect, you should do so even more so in addressing Deity.

Once the prayer is prepared, you should not simply memorize it and repeat it in rote fashion from the pulpit. But its contents should so grip your soul that you can truly utter it as a prayer. When Jesus gave his cry of dereliction from the cross (Matt. 27:46), he was not mechanically quoting Psalm 22:1 in order to fulfill prophecy. It had been prophesied, to be sure, but the cry came from the depths of his soul. This should be the nature of your prayer. You should so pray it that your prayer will stir the souls of the people and make your plea their own. Thus together you will stand before the throne of God's grace.

However, your sermon and invitation should prove to be the climax of the serivce. As you stand to preach, your very attitude should create a sense of expectancy in the hearts of the people. If you are adequately prepared in mind and heart, the Holy Spirit will give you what our forebears called "liberty." But there is a difference between self-assurance and cockiness. You should never forget that you are God's herald in things eternal and are totally dependent upon the Holy Spirit. You will be humbled if you have the spirit of Richard Baxter, who said that he preached as if never to preach again, as a dying man to dying men.

Your method of delivery will help or hinder the effectiveness of your message. It is necessary that you begin emotionally where the people are and endeavor to lead them to where you want them to be. I have seen some preachers come out of the *chute* like a whirlwind, as if they were fighting bees, and continue in that manner throughout the sermon. Had they been able to see inside their listeners, soon they probably would have seen the same fuss and fury within them. Other preachers are as tight as a bowstring. And most likely they soon have the congregation in the same condition. This is the reason why you should approach your message in calm assurance.

In preaching you should get your power volume not by over-working your vocal cords but by using your diaphragm and your stomach muscles. Vocal cords are small muscles which if abused will become tired. They will go limp, producing a husky or hoarse tone. This within itself will detract from your message. If properly used, your vocal cords become stronger as you preach. Thus you can better control your tones and make them more pleasing and effective as the sermon progresses.

At the outset of the message your style should be a lower tone and a slower tempo—not so low that you cannot be heard or so slow as to suggest that you are faltering in your thought processes. As you increase in volume and tempo your enunciation should be clear; words should never run together. Do not be a Johnny-one-note, but vary your tones. At any given point in your message the situation will determine whether you should shout or whisper. At times a whisper may be more emphatic than a shout. Slight pauses in delivery at times will serve as emphasis upon a thought. Any one tone—whether a shout or a whisper—if used constantly will not be emphatic at any point. As a musician uses loud, soft, and medium tones, so should you. It is the variation of tempo and tone which expresses emphasis. And as you speak your voice should reveal the note of earnestness, not a false tone simply to impress people, but one born out of genuine concern.

Many preachers face the problem of what to do with their hands while preaching. One thing you should not do is put them in your pockets. When I was in the seminary Mrs. A. T. Robertson had the custom of meeting at intervals with the wives of married students. She called these sessions "Please Tell Your Husband." Largely she dealt with pulpit manners. On one occasion she talked about the use of their hands, noting the bad habit of putting them in their pockets. She offered to give one of her books to the wife who broke her husband of doing so.

At the next meeting one told how she had succeeded. She began by talking to her husband about it so to make him conscious of the fact. When that failed she sewed up his pants pockets. But as he preached he kept pulling at the thread until it was removed. Then, in went his hands. Finally she succeeded by placing pins in these pockets with sharp points sticking upward. Each time he started to put his hands in his pockets they were stuck by the pins. After several Sundays of this he had gotten rid of a bad habit.

What can you do with your hands? Try holding your Bible in one and placing the other on the pulpit stand. Or place both of them there. At times clasp your hands in front of your body, but never behind you. But do not overdo this. Do not cross your arms and clasp them with the hands from the opposite side. And if you have any kind of ornament or jewelry such as a ring, do not play with them. And there is nothing wrong with simply letting your hands hang naturally at your sides.

In 1935, I was one of two students in the class chosen to speak at seminary graduation exercises. The previous day while Mrs. Hobbs and I were returning to Louisville from our church field, we were in a serious automobile wreck. Fortunately, no one was injured. But by nightfall every muscle in our bodies seemed to be as sore as a boil. I was still in that condition when I spoke on Tuesday evening. For twenty minutes I stood and spoke with my arms hanging at my sides. Afterward the principal of Woman's Missionary Training School raved to my wife about my posture. "Such poise! Such dignity! Not one time did he raise his hands!" When Frances told me about it, I said, "Honey, it was not poise or dignity. I was so sore I could not raise my arms." However, I do not recommend such extreme measures in order to use your hands properly!

But gestures with your hands and arms are perfectly proper if done wisely, gracefully, and in good taste. If you constantly whirl your arms above your head like a helicopter about to take off, the profuse gestures will be meaningless. It would be like shouting all the time. Helicopters take off this way, but it is not for preachers to *take off.* Arm and hand gestures should be used only when they illustrate or add emphasis. When used they should be done in a relaxed manner. This is especially true of your hands. They should be relaxed and gracefully extended. There may be times when you will want to point with a finger. But such should be done sparingly. At times even a fist held in front of you may demonstrate determination and power.

Many years ago a prominent pastor's son was called into the ministry. Up until this time he had been teaching in a university. He had had no training for the ministry. But his happy father invited him to fill the pulpit one Sunday evening. In his delivery almost from the first word to the last he kept pounding the pulpit Bible with his fist, as if he were driving a post into the ground. Later his father's only criticism was said in loving-kindness. "Son, you were called to *expound* the gospel, not *pound* it." Go thou, and do likewise! Why not stand before a mirror and practice various gestures of both face, arms, and hands. It will help to improve by seeing yourself as others see you.

It is important in preaching to begin with the proper pitch and tempo. The story is told of a sermon preached by John A. Broadus. He began his message at too high a pitch. So after a few minutes he stopped and said to his audience, "I regret that I began my message at too high a pitch. It is impossible for me to continue from there and reach the desired climax. With your gracious indulgence I will begin my sermon again."

Let us say that you have a sermon with three main divisions. The beginning of each should have its own pitch and tempo, the second and third being respectively increased. Each should be in keeping with the desired climax in that division. The second climax should be higher than the first, and the third higher than the second. The highest one should be conducive to the desired response toward which the entire sermon points. It should be a call to decision and action. Otherwise it leads nowhere. It will be like the rivers of Damascus. They originate in the mountains and flow merrily along through the city, only to be swallowed by the dry desert sands.

Sermons should close in such way as to lead naturally into the invitation. Failure to give an invitation leads to frustration. Those moved to a decision by the sermon have no opportunity openly to declare it. At the close of a church service a man who was the head of a large sales organization said to the pastor, "Pastor, that was a great sermon. But if you were a salesman of mine I would fire you." When asked why, he replied, "Because you made a good sales talk. We were ready to sign on the dotted line, but you did not give us the opportunity to do so."

The time of the invitation is the moment toward which the entire service has pointed. Therefore, time should be allotted for you to present it unhurriedly. It should be preceded by prayer that the Holy Spirit may have his way in the lives of those who are present. Following the prayer you should state clearly the invitation: to receive Christ; to identify one's Christian life with the local church fellowship; to surrender to God's call to a Christian vocation; to reconsecrate one's life to Christ. In order to avoid a break in the service, it is best for you to announce the invitation hymn. In order to avoid a loss of attention, this should be done after you have explained the multiple invitation. Instrumentalists should be instructed to be ready to begin playing the moment you request the people to stand. Any break in procedure at this point can mar the spirit of the moment.

From this point on procedures will vary. In large crusades Billy Graham stands with head bowed in prayer while the hymn is sung without interruption. In the smaller setting of a local church a word of encouragement is in order during the singing. You may do so more at length between stanzas. But remember that this is a time of pleading. You should never berate the people for not coming. As a lad on a farm I learned that you do not put a bridle on a horse by beating it over the head with it.

I find that during the invitation it is better to remain on the platform in full view. You can arrange for an associate, a deacon, or some other capable person to receive those who respond. By remaining on the platform not only can the people see you, but you can also see them. Thus you can determine the reactions in the congregation, especially if you ask for a show of hands. When I do this in order to avoid embarrassment, I first request everyone to bow their heads with eyes closed. Then I begin by asking members of the local church to lift their hands. From that point I proceed thus: those from other local churches who are visitors; Christians who are local residents with their church relationship outside the community; those who have never made a public commitment to Christ. At this point you should pray for all before proceeding.

For how long should you extend the invitation? This should be determined by the response. It should not be drawn out unduly unless there is a continual response. Somewhere I read about someone asking Dr. Truett if he had a rule as to how long to continue the invitation. He replied, "Yes, and it is very simple. When the Holy Spirit is working we dare not quit. When he is not we dare not presume."

Receiving those who come forward should not be a hurried affair. After all, this is the moment upon which all else centers. You should present each person individually with appropriate words. In the case of a husband and wife or a larger family group, each one should be brought forward by name and then all presented as a group. A word of explanation should be given as to the basis of each person's response. When this has been done for each one, then you should present the entire group to the congregation. It should be a time of rejoicing as members personally greet them (Luke 15:7,10).

Awesome Responsibility But Glorious Privilege

"Now then we are ambassadors for Christ, as though God did beseech you by us: we pray you in Christ's stead, be ye reconciled to God" (2 Cor. 5:20).

If you view being a preacher an awesome task, you are in good company. Paul faced his calling in the same way. In the above verse both "for" and "in stead" render a Greek word which means on behalf of or as a substitute for. As a preacher you stand in this relation to Christ. And your responsibility is to call upon lost people to become reconciled to God.

But if being a preacher is an awesome responsibility, it is also a glorious privilege. You and I are not only shepherds of souls but are responsible for how we discharge our office. Faithful performance is rewarded by divine praise. At best we are but earthen vessels. But if we do our best the Lord will see to the harvest.

8

Mind Your Manners!

Insofar as I know, neither Emily Post nor any other authority on etiquette ever included a chapter on how preachers should conduct themselves. Maybe they never thought that one was necessary. But preachers are human and are, therefore, subject to error. Since this is true perhaps some guidelines on ministerial conduct are in order. So at the risk of one black pot talking to other black kettles, here I go.

As social beings preachers have dealings with other such beings in the larger concourse of life. But in a special way they are related to other preachers. In both relationships they should mind their manners. I love preachers and stand ready to defend them against the barbs of criticism hurled at them by others. In a sense I am like the woman who said to another, "I guess I have the meanest kids on our block." The other replied, "Yes, I suppose you do." The mother said, "Now listen here. I can say that about my kids, but you can't." What she said was done in love. The other woman did not love them.

Now I do not set myself up as a father confessor or as a paragon of virtue. But from observation perhaps I can say some things which may be therapeutic medicine for some and preventive medicine for others. Whatever I say, I say it in love.

Preaching By Example

Many years ago one of my favorite comic strip characters was "Hambone," a black philosopher. One day he expressed a statement by Ralph Waldo Emerson in terms I could understand.

112

"What you do speaks so loud I can't hear what you say." Unless the life you live squares with your preaching, you will be just so much "sounding brass, or a tinkling cymbal" (1 Cor. 13:1). The basic personal asset you as a preacher have with which to do your work is your character. If that is besmirched then all other abilities count for nothing. Character is what you really are. Reputation is what people think you are. You reveal your character by what you do in the dark when no one else can see. If your character has a flaw, sooner or later it will come out. It is then that your reputation becomes a damaging thing.

In Ephesians 4:1 Paul exhorted his readers to "walk worthy of the vocation [calling] wherewith ye are called." The Greek word translated "worthy" carries the idea of scales or balances. In other words, your manner of living should be as heavy as or in balance with your calling or profession. And in Romans 2:21–22 the apostle asked some pointed and probing questions. "Thou therefore which teachest another, teachest thou not thyself? thou that preachest a man should not steal, dost thou steal? Thou that sayest a man should not commit adultery, dost thou commit adultery? thou that abhorrest idols, dost thou commit sacrilege" [or "rob temples"]? Continuing, he asked, "Thou that makest thy boast of the law, through breaking the law dishonourest thou God? For the name of God is blasphemed [spoken insultingly against] among the Gentiles through you" (vv. 23–24). "The law," of course, referred to the Scriptures. Thus this may apply directly to those who are called to interpret the Scriptures or to preach the gospel. If you live contrary to that which you preach you cause a lost world to look with scorn upon God himself. Even those who love the Lord will hold you in contempt. Thus your effectiveness as a preacher will be in direct ratio to the kind of life you live.

Conversely, if you live according to the Scriptures, your very life becomes the gospel bound up in human flesh. In the New Testament the word "conversation" refers to one's manner of living. Actually this archaic usage is not bad. In fact, it is very good. You *talk* as you *walk*. By your manner of life you tell the world the kind of person you are.

The story is told of Francis of Assisi saying to one of his pupils, "Let us go down to the marketplace and preach to the people." They walked through the marketplace without speaking a single word, and then returned home. The pupil said, "But, master, I thought we were going to preach to the people." Francis said, "We have, my son; we preached to them as we walked among them."

Moral Behavior

This phrase covers a wide range of conduct. Certainly you should be above reproach in this area of life. You should so deport yourself that even your good will not be spoken of as evil (Rom. 14:16). You should not become a hermit who withdraws altogether from the world. Paul wrote to the Corinthians "not to company with fornicators" (1 Cor. 5:9). But he hastened to add that he did not mean to stay entirely away from them and other sinners, "for then must ye needs go out of the world" (v. 10). Rather, you are to be among sinners, not partaking of their sins, but endeavoring to lead them to the Lord. The worst compliment (?) the worldly can pay you is to say that you are a "regular fellow, just one of us." You should not be a goody-goody, too pious to go where such people are, but you should not become a part of their kind of life. You do not need to lie down in the gutter with gutter rats in order to lift them up. Instead, you should stand on the curb as you extend a helping hand to lift them from the gutter onto the curb.

Jesus was censured by his enemies for being "a friend of publicans and sinners" (Matt. 11:19) because he dared to eat with them (Luke 15:2). However, "a friend of publicans and sinners" may read "of publicans and sinners a friend." Thus a criticism may become a compliment. But only if you do not become a participant in their sins. When in the home of Levi (Matthew) the scribes and Pharisees asked Jesus why he ate and drank with such. He reminded them that a physician is expected to be found where sick people are—not to take their disease but to be an instrument of healing among them. "I came," said he, "not to call the righteous, but sinners to repentance" (Luke 5:32). You should take your cue from the Great Physician of souls. Be in the world but not of it. You should never preach *down* to people. Rather, you should seek to identify with them in their need.

The story is told of a man on death row. Many preachers had tried to win him to the Lord by showing him what a great sinner he was and how greatly he needed to be saved. His only response was to curse and rail out at them. Finally, a layman asked if he might talk with the man. Entering his cell, he sat down on the cot beside him. Placing his hand upon his arm, he said, "You and I are in a bad fix, aren't we?" He soon had the man on his knees in tears praying that the Lord would save him.

As a preacher you should guard yourself against sexual impurity. I do not overstate the case when I say that this is the area in which you should be more alert than in any other. Failure at this point will wreck your entire ministry. Even if you are not guilty, indiscreet actions can open the door to suspicion and gossip, which can be almost as destructive.

As a pastor you have an entrée into homes which no other person has. Most home visitation is done during the day when a lady's husband is not at home. Even if neither you nor the wife entertain ideas of wrong conduct, the temptation is there nevertheless. For this reason some pastors ask either their wives or an associate to accompany them on such visits. As a general rule I have never done this, and certainly not for this reason. But I have always made such visits brief. Except in cases of illness I did not make regular visits to the same home often. And with rare exceptions I never did extended counseling in the home. Instead I requested that ladies come to my office. Even in such sessions in my office I kept the door open near my secretary's office.

Earlier I noted that in order to counsel people you must enter into their problems. However, in the case of the opposite sex you should not become emotionally involved. Such a condition is loaded with dynamite! Avoid any physical contact beyond a friendly handshake and, perhaps, a friendly pat on the back for encouragement when she leaves. On occasion an emotionally over-wrought woman may, literally, want to cry on your shoulders. In such case you should disengage yourself as gently and as soon as possible. And all the while you should pray that you may remain in control of the situation and of yourself. Yours is a spiritual ministry and not a physical one.

You recall what Jesus said about adultery being in the heart even if not in the body (Matt. 5:27–28). As I understand this lustful look, it means that one has already given the consent of his will. The overt act is prevented only because of lack of opportunity or fear of the consequences. This leads me to say that if you will guard your mind and heart from lust, you can also prevent it from taking charge of your body.

I can honestly say that in all my pastoral ministry I have never found myself in a dangerous situation in this regard. This leads me to raise a question. When a pastor does find himself in such a situation, is it because he either consciously or unconsciously, by word or attitude, invites such? Most women would hardly make such an approach to a pastor if she felt she would be rebuffed. At the same time, you should remember that a designing woman will find you choice game. Should such take place she knows you will not tell about it. And an evil woman will count you as quite a prize to hang in her trophy hall.

And another thing. Never take a lady member or lady members of your staff to lunch unless your wife is along. In all likelihood it is an innocent thing. But you throw yourself open to criticism if you do. Even to this day when I write a letter to some fine Christian lady, who is a close friend to Mrs. Hobbs and me, and close it with the mildest of endearing terms, I never sign my own name but sign it "The Hobbs." And in my expression of affection I always include both of us. This may seem to be an extreme. I think not. It is simply to keep above the level of suspicion.

A young ministerial student once asked Dr. Frank Tripp how he could have a successful ministry. Dr. Tripp replied, "Keep the finances up and get along with the ladies in the church, and you can stay as long as you wish." I do not think the latter meant to live on friendly terms with the Woman's Missionary Union. But whatever he meant, it remains that you should be friendly with the ladies but not become personally involved with any of them.

I cannot reasonably believe that a dedicated preacher or a real lady deliberately starts out with a view to illicit sex. It begins with little things which continue to build up until the situation gets out of control. "Behold, how great a matter a little fire kindleth!" (Jas. 3:5). A match carelessly used can burn down your house. You do not strike it with arson in mind. But suddenly your house is reduced to ashes. This can happen to your life.

Many years ago Wallace Hamilton published a book of sermons. The first one was entitled *Ride the Wild Horses*. He likened the emotions to wild horses. Instead of letting them run away and wreck your buggy, you should keep them under control so that they work for you. The sex or creative instinct is a wild horse. It has great power for good, provided you keep it under control and make it work in its God-intended channel. But if you let it get out of control it will destroy you. So "ride the wild horses" lest they become fiery demons of destruction.

Honest in Business

As a preacher you should never be involved in questionable business dealings. I have always questioned the wisdom of a pastor being involved in any business other than the King's business. I have known some who did—and some made a financial profit—but it was at the expense of their pastoral ministry and influence. (I am not referring to a preacher who must work at a job to earn a living, but one who is involved in efforts to make additional

118   PREACHER TALK

money when his church provides a livelihood.)

Like many preachers, I have had offers to buy stock in a new but speculative enterprise and to have my name added to the board of directors of the firm. Since I knew nothing about the business, the only earthly reason for such an offer was to use my name.

Some time after the Civil War an insurance company approached Robert E. Lee about electing him its president. He protested that he knew nothing about the business. They were honest enough to tell him they simply wanted to use his name. He replied, "My name is not for sale." Neither should yours be, provided you value it as you should.

One day two salesmen came to my office. They wanted to sell me some stock in a new real estate development adjacent to a new Baptist hospital. It just happened that they worked for two upright men whom I knew. I explained that as a matter of principle I did not invest in speculative enterprises. The next day they returned. This time they offered to give me five hundred shares of stock worth one dollar each. In return I was to arrange for them to have interviews with people in our church. For every sale they made they would credit my account with so much money until it paid for my stock. I said, "In other words, you want me to be your tout." They protested any such an idea. But I insisted that it amounted to this. Then I said, "It grieves me that you think I would sell my honor so cheaply. I was chairman of the committee which recommended that the hospital be located where it is, knowing that it would greatly enhance the value of adjacent land. Were I the kind of person you seem to think I am, I would quietly have bought several acres of choice land adjoining this property before our recommendation became public knowledge. I would now be a rich man.

"It just happens that I am a close friend of the men for whom you work. If they knew what you are doing, they would fire you in a second. Now you get out of my office, and don't you ever come back with such a proposition." Incidentally, these two friends to this day do not know of this. If they did, it would embarrass them to tears. *Do not ever sell your name or your influence!* No matter how high the price, it will be a poor bargain.

This matter of making money suggests another matter. As a preacher you should have a program for saving money for emergencies or for your retirement years. What I have said about "speculative" enterprises should not be applied to good stock. Since you are not versed in such matters it will be wise to consult a good investment counselor. His relatively small fee will be money well spent. Or you may invest in a mutual fund where your investments will be handled by experts in the field. You may want to invest in corporate or government bonds. Just remember that the higher the yield, the greater the risk.

Certainly you should buy life insurance as protection for your family. And you should do so while at an age when the premiums will not be too high. While my son was at home, in order to furnish maximum security for my wife and for him, I bought full-life-pay insurance. This enabled me to furnish them the most financial protection for a minimum of money. Recently a topnotch insurance man confirmed the wisdom of such.

As soon as you accept your first pastorate, get into your denomination's retirement plan. As noted previously, this matter should be settled before you accept a call to a church. If someone objects that this is not a spiritual approach, my answer is that God gave you a mind with which to think as well as emotions and a will by which to act. When you are young all this retirement business may seem out of place. But it is later than you think. You are not as far away from where I am as you think you are. Do not wait until the horse is out before locking the barn door!

A preacher should pay his debts. Your credit rating should be at the highest level. Granted that in some cases you may be underpaid. You may be like the man who said that his money ran out before the month did. But you should learn to live within your income. You should have a budget and live by it. If you lose your credit rating, you also acquire a bad reputation. I know that this is more easily said than done. But temperance in living includes more than not using alcoholic beverages! If you simply cannot make it on your present salary, perhaps you should talk with the finance committee about it. Should you move to another field, before leaving you should talk with any creditors you may have and assure them that you will continue to pay any remaining indebtedness. You should not leave behind even the possibility of a shadow concerning your honesty and reliability.

There may be times when you are the victim of unforeseen circumstances such as an expensive illness in your family. It may be that you will incur obligations on the basis of your anticipated income. And sad, but true, the church may fall behind in paying your salary. In any case you should consult with your creditors, informing them of the situation. If they know that you are sensitive to your obligations most of them will bear with you. But without that information they can only assume that you are careless about your obligations. It might in extreme cases be wise to consult with your banker about the possibility of borrowing enough money to pay your other creditors and thus be responsible only for prearranged payments to the bank which you can meet.

Speaking of a church not paying the pastor's salary, I had an interesting experience. A large church was considering me as its prospective pastor. Through their local credit orgainzation they made various and periodic inquiries about me and my family through the credit bureau of the city where I was then a pastor. It just happened that the head of our credit bureau was a friend of mine. He gave me progress reports from time to time. Frankly, some of their inquiries were infantile in nature and irked me. The telling blow was when they asked if I paid my debts on time. I was tempted to contact their credit organization, tell them that the church was considering me, and ask them to check to see if they paid the pastor's salary on time. But I did not yield to the temptation.

Finally another fine church called me. This was known to my friend. On Thursday this church's committee requested him to let them know if I would be in the pulpit the following Sunday. He told them they were too late, that I was resigning on Sunday to go to another church. Frankly, I question whether I should have gone to that church had they called me. What I knew about its committee could have affected my ministry there. But not nearly so much as where I was if I had not paid my debts on time.

Pastor to Pastor

Through the years I have admired physicians for their high standard of ethics in relation to each other. Pastors do not have a Hippocratic oath. But common Christian courtesy should be a sufficient guide for them in mutual relationships. The great Jewish teacher Hillel handed down what is often called the "Silver Rule." In essence he said that what is hateful to you, you should not do to another. What you do not want another pastor to do to you, you should not do to him. Jesus gave the highest rule of all, the Golden Rule (Matt. 7:12). Whereas Hillel's rule is negative in nature, Jesus' rule is positive. Applying it to the present theme, in effect it means that you should think of something good you would like for another pastor to do for you, then do it for him. Notice that Jesus preceded this rule with a lesson on prayer (vv. 7–11). It requires prayer and a double portion of God's grace for Christians to live by the Golden Rule.

I have never heard one doctor criticize another as to how he treated a patient or otherwise. But I have known some preachers who, while not *gossiping,* delighted in passing on juicy morsels of unwholesome information about another preacher. And like gossipers, I have never known one who, upon learning that his information was untrue, took the trouble of retracing his steps to right the wrong he had done! Incidentally, peddlers of such garbage usually know where the garbage cans are into which to deposit it. You should never allow your ears to become garbage cans!

Furthermore, one doctor will not meddle with another's patients. But, alas, many preachers feel no compunction of conscience in trying to lure another pastor's sheep into his fold. And somehow they seem to concentrate on the most active and capable ones. Imagine a doctor saying to a patient of another, "He has more patients than he needs. Why not let me treat you since I do not have a heavy practice. And, besides, you should use the doctors in your own neighborhood instead of going across the city to see another." And yet these are familiar arguments used by these sheep stealers. At times a church will start a mission, later organize it into a church, and even help it to finance needed buildings. But no sooner does the new church get started but its pastor begins working on the mother church's members. It is like a child eating its own mother! Now I am not simply pulling these examples out of a hat. I can document every one of them, and more, out of my own experience and that of others.

I will not use the man's name, since he is well known. But I heard him relate an incident about the pastor of a church recently organized by his church. The young pastor said, "As soon as we finish our new building I am going after your members who live in our area." The older pastor replied, "Well, I will tell you what I will do. I will give you a list of our members you can have if you can get them. If you do get them, we will not miss them and you will not know that you have them."

Speaking of the community where one lives, with modern transportation that could be anywhere in the greater metropolitan area of a city. Or it could cover large areas of a less congested region. To offset this argument someone drew up the slogan "Not the One Nearest to You but the One Dearest to You." If someone prefers to drive past your church and a dozen others to attend church where he wishes, that is his choice. It is not your business to seek to disturb him/her when there are lost and unenlisted people at your church door. A preacher's child asked him the difference between a convert and a proselyte. He said, "A 'convert' is when we get one of theirs; a 'proselyte' is when they get one of ours." Now in a large city there will be a natural flow of people from one church to another. But it should be by their preference, not your pressure.

I have known of some pastors who would not personally try to enlist in their churches members from another local church. But they encouraged their people to do so! They remind me of the Pharisees who insisted in doing *unlawful* things *legally*. If you want to see the title Jesus gave to such read Matthew 23.

An inner city church should minister to the people in its immediate surroundings. But if it be confined to that area, especially downtown churches, those people would hardly be able to finance the program the church provides for them.

Many years ago I went from a church in a large city to one in a comparably smaller city. On Saturday night before my first Sunday I received a phone call from a pastor. He reminded me that in a city churches should respect the areas of other churches. Then he proceeded to give me the boundaries of my field. After hearing him out I thanked him, and said, "But, Brother Blank, I seem to recall that Jesus said that 'the field is the world.' " End of conversation.

When I was pastor of Dauphin Way Baptist Church, the largest in Mobile, Alabama, one Monday morning at the pastors' conference one pastor giving his report said, "And we got one member from *Dauphin Way!*" I said, "That is fine, my brother. Have you taken any away from the devil lately?"

As pastor of a downtown church for almost twenty-four years I must confess that at times I felt like Nehemiah building the walls of Jerusalem. In one hand he held a trowel with which to build the wall. In the other he held a sword ready to ward off those who opposed him. He that hath ears to hear, let him hear!

Now these words may be rather straight talk, not *preacher* talk with the kid gloves of diplomacy. But in my judgment they need to be said. I feel that as one who has retired from the pastorate I am in position to say them. If in saying them I can help you and others, then I am happy to do so.

Ministerial ethics also should be applied in the relationship between the predecessor and the successor in a given pastorate. Other than the marriage relationship and that with one's children I know of no other human relationship that is so intimate and tender as that between a pastor and a church. And what God has joined together, let no man put asunder. Friction between predecessor and successor hurts the church and degrades the ministry. Two Christian gentlemen should avoid such. As the successor you should avoid such. As the predecessor you should not try to continue a pastoral relationship with your former church. If you wanted to keep on being its pastor, you should not have left it.

Now I realize that while you were the people's pastor, ties of love and reliance were formed. And without realizing it, the people themselves can aggravate the situation by wanting the former pastor to perform a wedding or conduct a funeral. As their former pastor you should not injure their feelings. But as the predecessor you should not make it more difficult for your successor by encouraging such. He must win the love and trust of the people. And he cannot do so with you trying to retain your hold on the people. You love them and they love you. But you can best show your love by continuing to be a friend and by encouraging them to love and follow their new pastor.

When I followed Dr. C. B. Arendall at Dauphin Way, the church called me one month before his retirement date. The Sunday following my acceptance of the call he said to the congregation, "You have called a new pastor who will be on the field January 1. So after December 31 I will neither bury nor marry any member of this church." After the service one dear soul came to him and said, "Dr. Arendall, when I die I want you to bury me." He replied, "Well, sister, then you had better die before December 31."

When I arrived on the field he came to see me. (Incidentally, when the church called me he was in the bed with the flu and was greatly disappointed that he could not be there to vote for me.) He said, "Now, pastor, I want to welcome you to the greatest church in the world. But I will not attend services here for quite a while. Most of the time I will be out of the city preaching. At other times Mrs. Arendall and I will attend church elsewhere. You must win the hearts of the people. And you cannot do so quickly with me hanging around."

Each week he came by to visit and pray with me. The first time he came to the study I offered him the chair behind the desk. He said, "Oh, no! That is the pastor's chair." The only problem I ever had with him was his constant refusal to assist me in funerals. His reasoning was that once he did it, there would be no stopping place. He only lived for fourteen months after his retirement. But his family remained in the church as long as I was there; two sons served as deacons. And the entire family gave me unswerving support.

When his son, Dr. Edgar M. Arendall, was considering going to Dawson Memorial Baptist Church, Birmingham, he came to me for counsel. By that time his father had died. He said that I was the nearest one to being his pastor. Dawson Memorial was at the time a very small church in a small fieldstone building located in a sparsely settled area of Birmingham. But the city was moving in that direction. I reminded him of words of his father. When he came to Dauphin Way it was a small church with a small red brick building. The Alabama Baptist State Convention was paying the interest on its debt to keep it from losing its property. Dr. Arendall told me that he had nothing but the opportunity. Twenty-one years later he retired, leaving the largest church with the largest Sunday School and the largest new auditorium paid for of any church in Alabama.

Then I said, "Ed, if you go to that church you too will have only the opportunity. But you will do what your father did in Mobile." It is now one of the greatest churches in the nation. Each year on his anniversary I drop him a note reminding him that he made a liar out of me. He has done a greater work in Birmingham than his father did in Mobile. And if his father were among us, he would say, "Amen!"

At the same time there must be the proper attitude on the part of the successor toward his predecessor. I do not hold myself up as a model, but I am speaking out of experience. To begin with, I visited and prayed with Dr. Arendall when he was ill during my precall visit to the church. Later I repeatedly asked for his counsel. At the first service as pastor I said to the church, "My family and I have not come to take the place of Dr. Arendall and his family in your hearts, but to make one for ourselves. The fact that you love them shows your capacity to love us. Do not be hesitant to show and express your love for them in our presence. Frankly, if after twenty-one years of service with them you did not love them, we would be afraid of you."

These words were spoken from the heart. But even had they been otherwise, they would have made good strategy. After the service the people crowded down to thank me for my words. And there was never a moment of friction caused either by the predecessor or the successor.

This was in 1945, while our nation was at war. The population of Mobile more than doubled as people came to this port city to work in the shipyards and other war-related industries. Many hundreds had joined the Sunday School. But since Dr. Arendall had announced the previous August his retirement plans, most of these waited until the church got a new pastor to decide whether or not to unite with the church. The result was that for the first six months of my ministry there an average of fifteen per Sunday united with the church, many of them for baptism on their profession of faith in Christ.

In July I wrote a brief article for the *Alabama Baptist* with the idea that the people generally would be interested in what the church was doing. After citing the above and other figures I stated that I was not foolish enough to think all this was happening because I was the pastor. It was but the fruit of the labors of the church under Dr. Arendall's leadership. It was the truth. And it proved to be a blessing by telling it. When Dr. John Jeter Hurt, Sr. read the article he wrote the editor expressing his delight over such "humility," and said I should be endowed and sent over the Southern Baptist Convention territory to tell pastors how to treat their predecessors. As Walter Brennan as the television character Will Sonnet was fond of saying, "No brag! Just fact!"

My good friend Chester Quarles read Dr. Hurt's letter in the paper. Then he wrote to tell me that there was not an humble bone in my body. I replied expressing my deep hurt that he should question my humility. Oh well! Preacher friends must have their fun!

I learned much from Dr. Arendall. So when I came to retirement from the pastorate, I tried to do it with as good grace as he did. However, I sought to strike a medium between extremes—the position Dr. Arendall took and that of some who continue to hold on to the people of a former pastorate. In my last Sunday morning sermon as pastor I told the congregation that as soon as they had a pastor on the field, I would perform no pastoral ministry to the congregation except by his invitation and that he must be included in occasions such as funerals and weddings. I would not render such ministries with him either sitting at home or else sitting in a pew. In the case of funerals I would deliver the eulogy if the family wished it, but he must be in charge. After the service several who had loved ones with terminal illnesses thanked me. One lady said, "I have wondered how I could have you for my husband's service without embarrassing the pastor, whoever he may be. You have provided the way."

My successor is Dr. Gene Garrison. When he arrived on the field the people respected my wishes. But some time later he said, "Pastor, I wish you would not require people to come through me to get you to do these things. If they want you just go ahead and do it. I understand the situation." I agreed, but with one stipulation. I would always notify him in advance of the service. Now after more than five years such calls come to me less and less. He has become the people's pastor. And this is as it should be.

Of course, there are close friendships which carry over into our new relationship. Just before my retirement one fine deacon said, "You will always be my pastor." I replied, "No, after December 31 I will no longer be your pastor. But I will always be your friend." In such cases where these are in the hospital or are bereaved I visit them. But I always make certain that the pastor has been there before me. If he is in the city I will not get there ahead of him. Shortly after the church called Dr. Garrison, Mrs. Hobbs and I deliberately arranged to be away for several months. It was our feeling that he and his wife needed the opportunity to get to know the people without our presence.

My pastor and I have the best of relationships. When I am in the city I usually drop in for a brief visit. He is too busy for me to monopolize his time. Never am I in a service but that in some graceful way he recognizes my presence. He has asked me to fill the pulpit more times than my schedule will allow—at times even when he is present. Whenever a major book of mine is published, he arranges to have an autograph party and reception for Mrs. Hobbs and me.

When we observed our golden wedding anniversary, the ladies of the church gave us a beautiful reception with the pastor's cooperation. Prior to the reception we had a service exactly like a wedding, except that we did not repeat vows we took fifty years previously. Instead it was in the form of a celebration. Dr. Garrison himself wrote out the service he would use. When he read it to us we asked him not to change one word of it.

Through his leadership my former secretary now serves as my secretary, along with other duties. Largely through my wishes, this to a great degree consists of typing manuscripts for books. We continue to live in Oklahoma City where we have put down our roots for over twenty-nine years. And the relationship between the Garrisons and the Hobbs could not be better!

Somehow people seem to expect trouble between a predecessor and a successor in a pastorate. This need not be the case. As Christian gentlemen they should be examples to the flock. Someone asked me if there had been any problems between us. I replied, "No, absolutely none! How could I respond adversely to such gracious treatment? As for my part, there has been no problem for three reasons. First, I have no desire to be a problem to him. Second, even if I did I am not at home enough to be one. Third, if I were still going to try to run the church, I would have remained on the payroll and been paid for my efforts." I do not think my mother ever dropped me on my head when I was small. If so, I was not very far off the floor when she did. In the words of another, "my mama did not raise any foolish children."

Another area in which ministerial ethics play a part is with regard to visiting preachers—evangelists or otherwise. When you have such you should see that he has a comfortable place to stay—if possible a hotel or motel with eating facilities. A basket of fruit in the room will prove most helpful in case he does not wish to eat a full meal. You should provide him with advance information as to name and address of the motel and as to what is expected of him while with you. If at all possible you should meet him upon his arrival and see that he is comfortably situated. Only when there is an extreme emergency should you send someone else to meet him. And it will prove helpful if you provide him with a typed schedule of his engagements while he is with you.

Most preachers never discuss finances with the host pastor before coming for an engagement. If one does without the pastor's request it is in bad taste. But this very fact places a burden of responsibility upon you as the pastor to see that he receives his expenses, plus a fitting honorarium. I have had the experience which I am sure is common to every preacher on occasion. Let us say that you invite another pastor to speak at a banquet. You have known for months or weeks in advance that he is coming. You should arrange to give him a check before he leaves, and it should take into account his expenses as well as an honorarium. Often on such occasions I have had pastors to say, "The treasurer is not here tonight to sign a check. I will mail it to you tomorrow."

There have been times when "tomorrow" meant anywhere from a week to a month later. Such an act tells me much about a preacher. One is that he does not plan ahead properly. This has never been my problem. But in some cases a pastor may sorely need the check in order to pay for a plane ticket or some other incurred expense.

Now just suppose that this preacher should call you at the last minute and say that it was inconvenient for him to come today, but he would be there the next day, week, or month. You would be justified in feeling that you had been done an injustice. It is just as great an injustice to him for you not to be prepared to remunerate him immediately after he has performed his service. Furthermore, he is your responsibility until you personally see him safely on his way home.

Through the years it was my policy in case of a revival to give a man his check before he left town, even if those responsible for the finances had to work overtime in counting the offering. The only exceptions were times when the evangelist left after the Friday night service and the bulk of the offering would come in the following Sunday or if he left immediately after the Sunday morning service before the money could be counted. In such cases, a check was mailed on Monday just as soon as the amount of it was determined. Also a *minimum* honorarium was agreed upon with the finance committee in advance, even if the love offering fell below that figure. I always tried to get the best preacher available and then remunerated him in kind. Frankly, I had too much pride in my church to do less than the best of our ability. I preferred giving a guest too much rather than too little.

You should see to it that all of the love offering goes to the evangelist. If it is customary to pay revival expenses out of it, it should be called a revival offering. But you should see to it that the evangelist gets every single cent above basic expenses, with some more added out of the budget if the amount is not sufficient. Not one cent of money designated as a love offering should be used for any other purpose. In a former pastorate a banker served on the church finance committee. In one meeting the committee was discussing using money for a purpose other than that for which it had been given. Finally the banker said, "If I ran my bank in this fashion I would be in the penitentiary."

A church invited an outstanding preacher to preach in a revival. In advance the pastor and finance committee agreed that the minimum honorarium should be $1,000. On the closing night of the revival the church was packed, with a large crowd standing in the vestibule and in the yard. Since the necessary amount of money was almost reached prior to this service, no appeal was made for money. But the plates were passed to receive an offering. When the finance committee counted it the amount of "loose offering" was $780.

After the crowd had departed the pastor went to the office, where the finance committee awaited him. He found them elated. One member said, "Pastor, we have enough money to give the evangelist the agreed amount and to put $500 in the building fund!" The pastor replied, "Not as long as I am your pastor. The people gave this money for our guest preacher, not for our building fund. I think he should receive all of it." Without one murmur of protest the committee agreed. The preacher received a check for $1,500, which was quite an offering for that time. He later told the pastor that this was the largest honorarium he had ever received for an eight-day revival.

This is a true story. How do I know? Because I was that pastor. I was no hero. For I knew that the committee would follow my suggestion. The committee members were not dishonest. They simply needed guidance. If we ask our people to be honest with God in their stewardship, we should be honest in the administration of that which is given. This principle applies to all church finances.

Speaking of revivals, a word is in order as to the manner of reporting immediate visible, numerical results. To begin with, *revival* refers to the saints. You cannot *re*vive something that has never been *vived*. If the church gets revived others will be reached—either during the *protracted* meeting or later. The real test of a revival comes later, not simply during specified dates on the church calendar.

Years ago my good friend, J. D. Grey, preached for us during such a week in Oklahoma City. I began the meeting on a beautiful Sunday when we had thirteen additions to the church. But from Monday night on through the following Sunday every service was rained out. Only the most faithful saints came. So naturally we did not have a single addition while J. D. was with us. When he was ready to leave he said, "Herschel, I will not tell people what a sorry church you have, if you will not tell them what a sorry evangelist I am." Of course, both of us have told it and laughed since about what was then a rather frustrating week.

In recent years it has become fashionable to report "decisions" during a revival without specifying what is involved. It is a dangerous practice! On one occasion I was in a revival not too far from Nashville, Tennessee. We were not having morning services. So early Tuesday morning I flew to Nashville to attend a committee meeting. I was asked how the revival was going. My reply was that we had already had five hundred decisions. Everyone was excited and wanted to know about it. I said, "Well we have had three services thus far. I estimate that we have had about that many total in attendance. Everyone had heard my sermons and had made the *decision* to go home and do nothing about it."

If you report "decisions" you should itemize them and identify the nature of each group. Otherwise this term can be misleading.

Denominational Relationship

While you are an individual who is ultimately responsible only to God you are also a part of a larger Christian fellowship, the denomination of which you are a part. And as such you should conduct yourself in a manner conducive to strengthening that fellowship. If you are a seminary graduate your theological education was made possible through the cooperative effort of the churches which made the seminary possible. For many of you the same is true of your college education at the state level. Experience has shown that local churches are most effective when they work cooperatively all the way from the local community to missionary endeavor on a worldwide scale. A large local church may at times feel that it is sufficient unto itself. But even it needs the fellowship of other churches. Furthermore, stronger churches should lend their strength to the weaker ones. As the pastor you should lead your church to be a cooperating one.

More to the point, you should not endeavor to lead out of the denomination the church of which you are the pastor. Sheep stealing is bad enough. But church stealing is worse by far. No denomination is perfect. But neither are you. The denomination's literature may not be perfect. But neither are you. If a church of a given denomination calls you as its pastor, it has the right to expect you to lead within its denomination framework. You have no moral right to do otherwise. If you see wrongs which need to be corrected, you should seek to do so from within, as a loyal member of the fellowship. But, I repeat, you have no moral right to steal a church from those with whom it has chosen to cooperate. If you cannot find a church to your liking, then start one from scratch. Do not seek to betray those who before you poured their lives into the making of a given church.

Even as you cooperate within your denomination you should avoid denominational "politics" as you would a plague. There are few things which degrade the ministry more than this. If you become bitten by this *bug,* you will find that the brethren are smarter than you think. Once you are recognized as one who seeks to maneuver for position or favor, you will most likely be denied the recognition for which you aspire.

It is natural for a young preacher to be ambitious. I would not give a dime for one who is not. But leave the matter in the hands of the Lord as he works through the brethren. When I first started out I thought that if I were ever appointed as a member of the obituary committee of the local association I would have it made. But after years in which I have been privileged to serve in almost every capacity my denomination could bestow, I have learned that it is largely a thankless task. It is a lot of hard work and endless hours in committees, sometimes stretching into the wee hours of the morning. Most of it is unknown to most, thus becoming a labor of love. Even when you perform publicly there will be those who say they could do it better. And they may be right. I have always taken the attitude that I am doing my best; if you think you can do better you are welcome to try. One in a responsible denominational position once said to me, "I have noticed that some people are always *running* for election to a position, but are never chosen. Usually there is someone who simply does his job. Then suddenly things begin to fall into place, and he is elected." So do the best you can where you are, and leave these other matters with the Lord. He will make his will known through the brethren.

A matter of broader import is that of your attendance and conduct at conventions. Pastors who attend usually have their expenses paid for by the church. When you are sent you should *go*. Recently I heard about a pastor who was fired by his church. The church leadership discovered that he had misused funds provided by the church for him to attend the Southern Baptist Convention. Instead, he used the money to take his family on a vacation somewhere else. Such is tantamount to stealing money from the offering plates!

Furthermore, if you go to the Convention you should attend the sessions. Your church does not send you to spend your time gassing with the brethren in the halls or elsewhere, or perhaps even going to a ball game, while the Convention is in session. You should attend whether or not you ever speak a word about involved issues. If you have something to say, say it. But do not become afflicted with *microphonitis* merely to gain publicity. When you attend you should pay attention to proceedings. I have seen messengers sit and read a newspaper while important business is being transacted or someone is speaking.

If you speak and/or listen you should do so in Christian love.

At times some brother will speak hard and heavy, loud and long in defense of the truth of the Bible. But he seems to forget one of those truths: "speaking the truth in love" (Eph. 4:15). Usually if Christians in such gatherings talk long enough they will talk themselves together. But even if a vote goes against your wishes you should accept it in Christian grace. This is usually the case if the brethren feel that they have had their say.

In short, at such gatherings you should conduct yourself in the same manner you want your people to do so in similar situations in the church back home: attend, listen, participate, vote, accept the will of the majority, and go away in love.

Thus, in considering "Mind Your Manners," we wind up where we started. "Therefore all things whatsoever ye would that men should do to you, do ye even so to them" (Matt. 7:12). In Christian relationships this Golden Rule is riches indeed!

9

Say "We"

The beautiful music of a pipe organ is produced by strong currents of air passing through the various pipes. Before electric motors were available this air was pumped by hand. In a certain case the pumping was done by a boy who worked hard but was never seen by the people hearing the organ. On one occasion an organist gave a recital. With skilled fingers and feet he delighted the audience with his playing. Time after time he stood and bowed to the applause of his listeners. All the while the little boy was pumping away behind the scene with no notice whatsoever from the audience or the organist.

After an unusual burst of applause and the bows of the musician he sat down to play again. But when he pressed the keys nothing happened. After adjusting certain gadgets on the console he tried again. But still no sound. Following several futile attempts the organist heard a sound "Psst, psst" coming from the corner of the platform. He saw the boy peeping around the drapes with an impish grin on his face. Then he said, "Say 'we,' mister; say 'we!'" He was tired of doing all the hard work without any recognition.

This might well be a parable of a pastor and his staff. So often he stands up and takes the bows for successful accomplishments in the church program when the really hard work is done in the background by the church staff which receives little or no recognition. So, brother pastor, if you listen carefully you may hear a "psst" coming from your staff as in their minds they are thinking, "Say 'we,' mister; say 'we!'" And in all honesty, your role as the pastor may succeed or fail in keeping with your relations to and attitude toward your staff. This is true whether the "staff" consists of many people or only of a church secretary, a paid janitor, certain volunteer workers, or of numerous people who follow a full-time Christian vocation.

Aids to Greatness

Many years ago I wrote a little book called *Moses' Mighty Men*. It consisted largely of a study of the principal characters who aided Moses in his work. Its thesis was that it requires three things to make a great man. He must be endowed with the qualities of greatness; he must be placed in a historical environment which calls forth his greatness; and he must be surrounded by lesser greats who contribute to his greatness. Select any great man in history or now living, and these factors will apply. They certainly apply in your case as a pastor.

No matter how innately gifted you may be, how well-trained you are in your particular field, or how great the challenge and opportunity of the present may be, you simply cannot do everything. Time and energy place a limit upon your activities. At the same time there are needed skills which you do not possess. The only answer to your problem is to enlist or engage other people who can supply your lack. I am thinking primarily of the building and use of a staff of people who have been called of the Lord to develop and use their own abilities in his service.

One man can minister adequately only to a certain number of people. Somewhere I read that when the membership of a church passes the one thousand mark a new assistant pastor is needed to help carry on the ministry, and that the same is true for every thousand member increase thereafter.

You may be able to preach like Spurgeon, yet not be able to carry a tune in a mail sack with the lock on it. For this reason you need a minister of music whether paid full time, part time, or voluntary. Even smaller churches need a minister of education and the necessary secretarial and caretaker staff. Larger churches should have workers for the various age groups. Of course, the church's financial strength will be a determining factor in the number of staff members your church can afford. However, it has been my experience that where a need exists, if you get the proper person to fill that need the increase in financial receipts will offset the cost. Where necessary you can find a combination man to serve as music-education director.

At one place during my pastoral ministry we had such a combination man. But the Sunday School was of such size that we needed supervisors over various age groups. Unable to afford paid workers for these positions, we selected volunteer workers to serve as supervisors over the other voluntary workers in these groupings. It served well until the church could afford to secure professionally trained personnel for these positions. For purposes of administration and promotion they were regarded as staff members who were included in all planning and promotion meetings. However, the primary need is not so much how many staff members you have but their ability, training, dedication, and how they are used.

Staff Selection

The policy in securing staff members will vary from church to church. In some cases you may be invested with the authority to do so. Other churches may have a personnel committee which is charged with that responsibility. This is one of those areas in which there should be a clear understanding before you accept the call to a church.

Should you be given this authority, you will be wise to consult and work with any church committee which is related to a given area—for instance, in selecting a minister of music that group would be the music committee. In cases where a church has a personnel committee, of course you should work with and through them. But even there this commitee should consult with any other church committee involved in that area. If for no other reason, it is common courtesy. Since you are the one to work directly with the staff member, your wishes certainly should be taken into consideration. In all likelihood the committee will ask you to suggest people to be considered. In the final decision it should be one with which you concur. It should be made clear to the person as to whom he is responsible. Normally it would be the pastor. Matters of a financial nature should be cleared with the finance committee except in those cases where the church has already adopted a budget which stipulates this item. But in any case you should keep the finance committee informed.

In the selection of staff members two things are of primary importance. You should take time to find the right person for a position. And you should seek out people who will complement your own ministry.

You should never act hastily in selecting a staff member simply for the sake of filling a position. Sometimes pressure from well-meaning members may tempt you to do this. But you do not want to make the mistake of getting someone who will fill the position but not meet the need. So long as the vacancy exists you can still be looking. But if you get the wrong person you must wait until that person moves before finding the right one. Once a person is secured time is necessary for him/her to get acquainted with the people and program before functioning efficiently. Thus a mistake in the first place only doubles this necessary period of time. In such case the old proverb applies that haste makes waste. On the other hand, patience in finding the proper person will pay off in the long run.

Furthermore, you should seek someone whose ability will make up for your lack of it in given areas. Since you are to fill the pulpit, you do not need another pulpiteer for an assistant pastor. If you select someone who has both the ability and desire to preach, you create a potential trouble area between you and him. It would be better for such a person to have a church of his own. Instead you should find a preacher who prefers visitation and personal soul winning over preaching.

A valuable source for information about prospective workers is seminary professors who are in a position to give you suggestions and evaluations. They may suggest some student who is graduating or someone on the staff of a church. In the final analysis, however, the choice should be yours. A person who is good for one church may or may not be good for yours.

If you are in need of an assistant pastor, many seminaries have intern programs whereby a graduate spends about two years with a church. They both serve and also learn the operation of a church program. Should you be in a church near a seminary and also have limited financial resources, you might consider a student on a part-time basis. One of the most fruitful years for me was when during graduate studies at the seminary I served as assistant to Dr. T. D. Brown at the Highland Baptist Church, Louisville, Kentucky. As I assisted him I both observed him and his work, and was brought by him into the inner workings of a city church with an active program.

Many retired pastors who are in good health are available for part-time service at a salary figure permitted by Social Security, as are other pastors not yet retired, but who would like to be free from the heavier burdens involved in being a pastor. These could serve full time at full salary. I know from experience that such can be a blessing to the church and the church to them.

With regard to selecting someone who can fill your lack, this is perhaps most important in the securing of a minister of education. This person should be someone with an open, friendly personality, capable, cooperative, able to work with people on the staff and in the membership, dedicated, and with the ability to work with details. Most of you are like I am. I delight in helping to formulate policy, viewing the program as a whole, and promoting it where necessary. But I do not like to be enmeshed with details. Obviously, therefore, I needed someone who was gifted in that area. Most people in the educational field have this ability. However, you should be certain that the person under consideration does have that gift. Otherwise you handicap yourself and the work.

In dealing with a prospective worker there should be a clear understanding as to the duties involved. Also as to the privileges such as remuneration, housing, moving expenses, retirement program, vacation, time off for encampments and/or other engagements away from the church. As with the pastor, these things should be put in writing—including a job description. This will put the worker at ease and avoid the possibility of misunderstanding later on.

Now let us suppose that you are going to a church which already has a staff of workers in the various areas. It has been my experience that you will be wise to retain it. If not, you will start out by having incurred resentment on the part of segments of the people, for each staff member will have friends in the congregation. If you change the staff in whole or in part you will find yourself handicapped from the outset. If in your judgment changes are needed, that can be done later after you are established in the hearts of the people. You may find that the existing staff is the very one you desire. And with their knowledge of the people and program they can prove to be of great value in assisting you as you become acquainted with the church and its needs.

As the work grows you may find it necessary to enlarge your staff personnel. For instance, you may need to add age-division supervisors in the educational program. In my own practice I had the minister of education in counsel with me to do the bird-dogging. After all, he knows the prospective workers in that area better than you do. Also since he will work directly with the person, he should be involved in the selection. Once he and I agreed on someone that person was invited to visit the church. Once the minister of education is satisfied that the person is the one wanted and is available, a meeting should be arranged for him to get acquainted with the key people in the area of service involved. Be certain to include the education committee. If this response is favorable, then matters may be finalized with the prospect. But before the matter is fully decided, as the pastor, you should visit with him. This will dignify the position and also enable the two of you to have an understanding as to your relationship. As the pastor you should present the person's name to the church for voting on your recommendation, if that is necessary. Otherwise, you should simply announce that this person is coming to work with them.

Sadly, at times it may be necessary to remove a staff member. This should never be done in anger. And it should be as a last resort. You bear a dual relationship to your staff. In a sense on behalf of the church you are their employer. But you are also their pastor. As the former you cannot be true to the church's trust in ignoring the need for a change. But as the latter it should be done with a shepherd's heart in such fashion as not to seriously injure the sheep. Unless moral issues are involved you should not dismiss a staff member outright. But you should talk with him as a pastor and friend as to the need for a change—one which in most cases will be beneficial both to the person and to the church. It may be that the church is unhappy with the staff member's work. If allowed to continue it could reach the explosive state, causing harm to all involved.

Time should be allowed for this person to find another place of service, then a resignation can be offered in dignity. It is far better to allow time for a peaceful solution than to act hastily, and then have to spend more time alleviating resentment toward you by those in the church who will not agree with your action. For the most part you will find that in good grace the church will accept a resignation, and that you and the former staff member will remain friends.

In other cases some staff member whom you regret losing will speak to you about resigning to go elsewhere. If it is due to unhappiness over working conditions or the like, you can always seek to remedy the situation. But in my judgment you should not offer that person a salary increase in order to dissuade him from leaving. You should not try to buy the person's will. But should he on his own decide to remain, you should see to it that he receives a salary increase commensurate to that he would have received elsewhere. No staff member should be asked to pay for the privilege of working with you and the church.

It was my policy in the conference with a prospective staff member to state that if he ever said that his leaving was the Lord's will, he tied my hands. I could only offer my best wishes and prayers. As a pastor you live by the Lord's will. Therefore, you should never try to persuade anyone else to act contrary to it. On more than one occasion I have said, "I say it with tears. But since you feel that God is leading, you should go. That is a matter between you and the Lord, not between you and me."

Staff Organization

It is a principle of physics that two objects cannot occupy the same space at the same time. More picturesquely, if two people ride the same horse at the same time, one must ride in front and the other behind. In terms of a church staff, the pastor and any other staff member cannot be on equal footing in terms of authority. By the very nature of things one person should be head of the staff—the pastor. Otherwise, the result will be pandemonium.

It naturally follows, however, that it is your responsibility as pastor to provide a plan of staff organization. You will be wise to consult key staff members in doing so. But ultimately the decision is yours. Even in the simplest of staffs each one involved should know the scope of his responsibility. Should you have a multiple staff composed of several people the same is true. But should you eventually find yourself with a complex staff personnel, organization is even more important. Each person should understand the area of his duties and the one to whom he is responsible. Without such an understanding you will find yourself overloaded with administrative details. You will wind up being the referee of differences rather than being the pastor of the flock. And since you are not made of iron, you will be riding to a nervous breakdown and total physical collapse. Even of greater importance, the Lord's work will suffer as a consequence. On the other side, plain common sense will provide you with a happy and effective staff which leads in a fruitful work.

In Oklahoma City we had a staff of over forty people. As the pastor I was the head of the staff. The assistant pastor and the pastor's secretary worked under my direct supervision. In addition we had four department heads: ministers of education, music, business administration, and activities (mainly recreation). Each of these was responsible to me. Under the department heads were those, including secretarial workers, who were directly related to their work. These were respectively responsible to the head of their department. As stated earlier I delegated both responsibility and authority to each department head. In turn each of these did the same to those in his department who worked in a supervisory capacity. Within departments each person—including secretarial and clerical help, kitchen services, and building and grounds maintenance—knew what his/her assigned responsibilities were. This prevented overlapping and promoted efficiency. Under this system only six people were directly responsible to me. And yet the "chain of command" was distributed throughout.

A person can work for only one boss. For example, in the department of business administration the building engineer worked under the business administrator and the janitorial staff worked under the building engineer. With that arrangement I never corrected a janitor with regard to his work. Neither did I consult the building engineer about it. I took the matter to the business administrator and let him handle it through the proper channel of responsibility. Nor did I tell a janitor what to do at a given time. He may have been told by the building engineer to do something else at the same time. So he would be placed in a dilemma. Such can be avoided if you respect the channel of responsibility and authority you have set up. Of course, in a situation where one man was assigned the responsibility for seeing that the chapel was ready for a funeral or wedding, I felt free to tell him to do whatever needed to be done. But I am talking about routine operations.

I might add that in a staff organization someone should be

designated to be in charge should the pastor be away. Since his work usually covers a broader range of activity than others', perhaps the minister of education is the logical one for this. Furthermore, should two department heads have a problem between them which they are unable to solve, the two should bring it to the pastor. Or if one such exists within a department, say, between an age-group supervisor and the minister of education, they also should bring it to the pastor. Complaints by one staff worker about another should be handled only with both parties present. As the pastor you should not be involved in every little detail. But everyone should know that you are in charge and are available when necessary.

In the matter of making the best use of your staff let me relate an experience. So often your staff is regarded by the members in relation to a routine duty. To enlarge their usefulness and enhance this relation to the people we worked out a program in which the department heads assisted me in hospital visitation. This even included the business administrator. Each was given a day in which to do this. Of course, this did not lessen my own visiting in this area. But it enabled the people to see these men in a new light, and bound them to the people in specific ties of love. For instance, instead of regarding the business administrator as someone trying to get money out of them, they saw him as one who cared for them in their need. It also proved to be a blessing to the men themselves as it added a personal dimension to their ministry.

Staff Meetings

If such an organization is to work efficiently, regular staff meetings at a fixed time are absolute necessities. In case of emergencies between staff meetings you should be accessible to any department head. But if it can wait it should be brought up in staff meeting. These meetings should be held without fail. If the pastor is out of town or involved in some ministry such as a funeral, the one designated to take charge should do so.

Actually in our church we had two staff meetings per week. I found that Monday and Tuesday mornings the staff was busy with necessary things such as preparing copy for the church paper and counting and banking money. (Speaking of paper copy, various items should be assigned to certain people. The pastor should have equitable space, but not monopolize the available space at the expense of other items. Usually the minister of education and his secretary should do the final editing and layout work.) So we had a meeting of the promotional staff on Wednesday morning, followed by a meeting which included the secretarial staff and others related to the overall program such as the church hostess and the building engineer. The secretarial staff should be aware of what is going on. It does not make a good impression if some member calls to inquire about some phase of the program only to be told "I don't know."

Staff meetings should begin on time! And, unless hindered beyond a person's control, each one should be expected to be on time. I read somewhere about a committee meeting involving Dr. Truett and five other men. One was five minutes late. Dr. Truett said, "Brother Blank, I regret that you have wasted twenty-five minutes of our time." When he said he was only five minutes late, Dr. Truett said, "Yes. But there are five of us who have waited."

Whenever a person was added to our promotional staff I told him/her that we wanted people who felt free to use their own minds, dreams, and vision in planning the work. Thus in staff meetings each person was expected to come with *input* for the session—not some far-out idea but something on paper to share with others.

In conducting a staff meeting, as the pastor you may want to begin by presenting your ideas on future programs to be considered at a later time. Thus the staff can be thinking of suggestions regarding such an undertaking. But with regard to current activities you might want to reserve your comments until all others have spoken. In this way you will not cramp their style but enable them to speak freely. In the course of the meeting each person should be given a brief time to report on accomplishments and about plans for action in implementing current programs. After this you may add comments of your own, and lead in a general discussion of the work of all phases of the present and of approaching programs.

Values inherent in such meetings include prevention of conflicts in the stated events of the various departments; a cross-fertilization of shared ideas; the molding of all efforts toward a common goal; and the shaping of the staff into a cohesive force in which each person is encouraged to become a part of a team rather than to have fragmented groups running in all directions and at cross purposes with each other. One overriding value is that it enables you as the pastor to see the program as a whole, to know what is being done, and to enable you to throw the weight of your position behind worthy efforts which need your help and influence.

Staff Fellowship

For a staff to be effective it should enjoy a spirit of good fellowship. I use the word "fellowship" in the New Testament sense of sharing or having all things in common. There should be the sense that "We are all in this work together" and that what benefits one benefits all. As the pastor you should discourage the formation of cliques within the staff. Through your leadership you should avoid one department being arrayed against another. You should seek to gather about you team people rather than stars or prima donnas. The staff should be led to pray together, play together, and stay together. It has been my experience that if the staff sticks together they can endure any adversity which they may confront. But if they become divided each one is a sitting duck for any disgruntled member or group of such.

Loyalty is a primary factor in fellowship. A sermonette along this line is appropriate at intervals in staff meetings: loyalty to the church, to the program, and to each other. In my conference with prospective staff members I always stressed this fact. I even made it personal. I always said: "I will overlook shoddy work to a fault. But I will not tolerate disloyalty for one minute. I will be loyal to you and I expect the same from you." Seldom did I discover even a trace of a breach of trust.

Sharing involves the pastor's respect for and support of his staff members as they work under his direction. If a staff member under my direct supervision was at fault I talked with him privately. You should never embarrass a staff member by criticizing him/her in the presence of others.

There were times when a staff member would encounter difficulty with some member or members as he promoted a program on my behalf. In such cases I always supported the staff member. If he had made mistakes we sought to correct them together. If compromises were necessary we made them together. To use a football term, at times I would throw a block while the staff member carried the ball. Never did I let a staff member suffer for me while I looked on silently, doing nothing to help.

There may be negative forces in the church which will tackle a staff member, but will not take on the pastor. On one occasion in one of my pastorates the church had voted to adopt a certain program. But there were some who opposed it. The minister of education was carrying the ball for me. I learned that this opposing group was circulating a petition asking the church to fire him. Through a friend I sent word that I was aware of the petition. And I requested that they write my name just above his. My reasons were stated as follows. "In the first place, the church will not do what you ask. In the second place, the church by its own volition authorized me to employ and dismiss staff personnel. Until it rescinds that action I intend to bear the responsibility. As the situation now stands, even if the church did do what you wish it would be voting to accept my resignation at the same time. Thus you might as well place my name at the top of the list." That was the last I ever heard of that petition.

Fellowship also calls for the pastor to associate with the staff in other than official duties. You should at times come out of

your "ivory tower" and be one of them in social fellowship. I
am not thinking about taking any one man as your golf or fishing
buddy. This would only serve to separate you from the other
men. And even if you rotated among the men, what about the
ladies? I am talking about your being a human being. Why not
on occasion drop by their offices or desks to ask how they are
getting along? Ask about the wife/husband, children, or parents.
Let them know that you are interested in them as people, not
merely as staff members. Be a pastor to them instead of just a
boss. Do not do this routinely but personally. You should not
simply go from person to person as though it were a planned
thing. Let it be on a drop-in or by-the-way basis.

One of the best ways to have fellowship with the entire staff
is to join them at coffee break time. In our church the coffee
wagon was brought to the office at 10:00 A.M. and 3:00 P.M. In
the morning a period of fellowship was followed by a time of
devotion and prayer. I always made it a point to be present for
at least one of these times each day. I found that on a day-to-
day basis I could get closer to the staff at these times than at
any other. By all means do not remain in your office during such
times. Or come out for a cup of coffee and take it back into
your office while the others have these brief times of fellowship.
Be one of them for the time. You will find that these moments
pay great dividends in personal relations with the staff.

Each year shortly before Christmas the entire staff had a dinner
at church expense. Following a steak dinner we went to our home
where Mrs. Hobbs served dessert and coffee—although most of
the group preferred her punch made by her own secret recipe.
After this we exchanged gifts. These were made possible by having
drawn names prior to this night. The gifts were inexpensive, usually something funny. These were placed under the Christmas
tree. The people were like children on Christmas morning as they
waited to hear their name called. After this hilarious time Mrs.
Hobbs and I spoke a brief word of appreciation for the staff.
The gathering was closed with prayer. They looked forward to

this time in our home even more than they did to the steak dinner. Nothing we ever did exceeded this in making the entire staff a family—our family.

Staff Recognition

Since staff members are human they like to receive recognition for a job well done. The least you can do as the pastor is to express your appreciation privately and/or in staff meetings. But it should go beyond that.

One man did another a favor. The recipient of it said, "I wish there were some way I could express my appreciation to you." The other replied, "Well, since the Phoenicians invented money they have not improved on that."

One way by which both you and the church can show appreciation for staff members is through annual increases in salary. They do not work for the church simply for money. If that were their primary objective they would probably be in other employment. But they do have expenses and need their remuneration. Certainly the constant rise in cost of living calls for a commensurate increase in income. Otherwise failure to equal this increase is actually a reduction in salary. If it equals that and nothing more, they are at a standstill. So the increase should be for a percentage beyond the increase in living costs. The cost of living increase is simply enabling them to keep up with inflation. All above that is one way of saying, "We love and appreciate you and your work." Such a pat on the back will amount to a small sum in monetary cost. But it will increase staff morale, resulting in more enthusiastic work.

If a staff worker is having monetary problems he certainly cannot give undivided attention to the work. Thus through no fault of his the work suffers. This can be prevented by a fair consideration of the person's needs. In most cases the pastor is expected to suggest salary increases to the budget committee. Of course, your own salary should be left up to the committee.

I have known instances where failure to increase salaries resulted in staff members being forced to move to another place which offered a higher salary. Recently I read an article about pastors' salaries. It was headed "Long Pastorates Tend Toward Low Salaries." Where a pastor remains in a church for many years, the brethren are unaware of the increased salary scale. But once they go looking for another pastor they are in for a rude awakening. In order to secure the kind of pastor they need they must pay far more for a new one who knows absolutely nothing about the church, whereas the previous pastor had given them the benefit of long years of experience at a lesser salary.

The same is true of other staff members. Rather than to increase the salary of proved, experienced people, the church lets them slip away. Then they must replace them at a much higher salary with someone who does not even know his way to the church building. This is not only poor Christianity but worse business administration!

In our work seldom will a staff member request a salary increase. It is your responsibility as the pastor to see that your staff is taken care of financially. You should keep abreast of the salary scales and lead your church to do fairly by those who serve with them. By doing so, you may even make the brethren aware of what is happening in the area of pastors' salaries.

Some churches have an annual "Staff Appreciation Day." This is fine provided it does not become a mere formality. But even this cannot suffice for your own expressions of appreciation for work well-done. In addition to private, personal expressions, you should do so publicly. Let the people know about their devotion to duty. Where some program succeeds because of the devoted service of any one or all of them, give public recognition of that fact. This can be done through the church paper, from the pulpit, and on other fitting occasions.

This should not be confined to the promotion staff or those who make public appearances before the people. Do not forget the church kitchen staff. Remind the people that the comfortable building and other appointments are no accident, but are the work of the building overseer and janitorial staff. Each person should be recognized for the part played in a well-ordered program. And do not forget "Bezaleel."

It is so easy for the pastor to accept the plaudits and take the bows for successes in the church program. One day the minister of education showed me the column of a pastor in another church paper. He had encircled with a red pencil the personal pronouns used. Honestly, it looked almost like he had spilled a bottle of red ink over it. I am sure this pastor was not aware of this egotistical display. It is a hidden trap into which any pastor may fall if he is not careful.

So "Say 'we,' mister, say 'we.'" Or you may find yourself in a position in which you cannot even say "I."

10

You Can Take Them with You

Two ministers of education were talking. The previous evening the church where one of them served had for the time being dropped consideration of a new program in which he was deeply interested. The decision was reached due to strong opposition on the part of a small but vocal group. The other asked him, "Are you going to leave?" He said, "No. Why should I? If I moved I would have to learn who they are there."

His reply was one of wisdom. For no one church has a monopoly on problems. This is a lesson which you as a pastor should learn. And the earlier in your ministry that you learn it, the better it will be. The Lord has promised to lead us in times of trials. But sometimes the only way out is through. If you run from problems where you are, not only will you lose confidence in and respect for yourself; you will also find the same or similar problems wherever you may go.

As a young pastor attending the state or national conventions, I would hear my contemporaries talk about the great things happening in their churches. But I do not recall one time when anyone spoke of the problems confronting him. However, as I listened I did think of the problems I was facing. Often I would return home thinking that I alone had such situations. Since then I have learned better. But I must confess that at times I returned home discouraged. At that stage in my ministry I did not realize that my friends also had problems, only, unlike myself, they did not talk about them on such occasions.

It is said of money that when you die you cannot take it with you. But if you move from one church to another simply to get away from problems, you will find that you can take them with you and/or you will find them waiting for you when you arrive.

Source of Problems

Wherever you find people you find problems. For people are problems. The only person who is free from problems in social relationships is one who dwells alone on a deserted island. If you have two people on this island you will have problems. If you add a third person the problems can multiply beyond counting. You can see, therefore, how futile it is to try to run away from them.

Yes, you can take them with you. Which implies that you yourself can be a problem or the source of such in your church. It may rest in your attitude. You may be opinionated. Or you may have a martyr's complex which causes you to have what Lum and Abner, two rustic radio characters many years ago, called "A case of the sorrowfuls"—feeling sorry for yourself. You may tend to be dictatorial which incurs resentment when "sweet reasonableness" would serve far better. You may regard honest differences of opinion about some matter as an attack upon you or your leadership.

You may become a problem by neglecting pastoral duties. I am honestly concerned about a growing attitude among some of the younger generation of preachers, a concern held by many of us oldsters—both pastors and laymen. It is the attitude of not being involved in pastoral visitation and other ministries and administration, but spending all one's time in the study. I should not be either/or but both/and. Your people will overlook your many mistakes and shortcomings, but they will not overlook neglect on your part in times of their needs. And rightly so! They may remain silent but the resentment is there. And this will even lessen the effectiveness of the sermons you so carefully prepare while your sheep feel that they have a preacher but no shepherd.

I repeat what I said earlier. You can preach *at* your people on Sunday without being with them during the week, but you cannot preach *to* them. You can say anything to your people from the pulpit, even dressing them down, and they will not resent it—if they know that you love them. But if they do not see evidences of love, then often they will read into other sermons a hostility you may not feel. Eventually these things can create problems with regard to your relationship to the church and its program.

A man came to me with a problem in his relationship to others in the church. I knew that the problem really was in his own attitude. When he told me he was going to move his membership, I said, "I speak in all kindness. You can do as you plan. But when you walk down the aisle of another church and take your seat on the front pew, do not think you have left your problem behind. In fact, you will have taken it with you. For your problem is within yourself." The same advice applies to some preachers.

On the other hand, the problems may be centered in others. There are some people who are just plain ornery. I have known some who felt they were called to oppose the preacher and other church leaders. But these should be a test of your Christian love and patience. In the words of one of my seminary professors, you must love your people—warts and all. And every church has its *warts*.

However, problems may arise through honest differences as to certain facets of the church life. In such cases you must be firm in your leadership but not to the point of running roughshod over opposition. Instead you should endeavor to lead different factions to a meeting of minds. Unless moral principles are involved, compromise is far better than conflict. This may involve compromise on your part. It may be that at certain points your opposition is right and you are wrong. You should never feel that your leadership is at stake if you do not always have your way.

Somewhere I read an article on honesty in the pulpit. One example of dishonesty cited was for the pastor to say from the pulpit that the Lord was leading him in a certain enterprise, when it was actually a matter of getting his own way. If you really feel that the Lord is leading you, then pray that he will show you how to achieve the purpose through amicable agreement rather than through tyrannical fiat.

The only time you are justified in leaving a church because of problems is when you are the issue to the point that should you remain it would result in splitting the church. Should that be the case you should encourage your friends in the matter to remain with the church fellowship, lead in a spirit of mutual forgiveness, and get on with the work. On the other side of the coin, I have known of pastors who led a disturbing element to form a new church with them as pastor. In most instances they lived to regret it, for the bad spirit which produced the division is carried over into the new church. And more often than not, the pastor eventually had to leave anyway.

Yes, you can take your problems with you. It will bear repeating that even if you run from them in one place, after a brief "honeymoon" you will encounter them again. Because you will find the same kinds of people where you go as were in the church you left.

The story is told of two incidents in the pioneer days in the Western United States. One day a man came by a cabin in his wagon. The owner of the cabin asked where he was going. He said he was looking for a place to settle where he would have good neighbors. "What kind of neighbors do you have around here?" he asked. In return he was asked what kind of neighbors he had at the place from which he came. He replied, "They were the meanest, most unfriendly people you ever saw." "Well," said the settler, "you will find the same kind of people here." So the man drove on. Later that day another man drove by with the same purpose in mind. Eventually the settler asked what kind of neighbors he had back home. Said he, "They were the nicest, friendliest people you ever saw." To which the settler replied, "Well, you will find the same kind of people here." So the man picked out a piece of land, settled, and found it to be true. Do you get the message? There may be exceptions to this story, but not many. "A man that hath friends must shew himself friendly" (Prov. 18:24).

Facing Problems

Of course, the best way to face problems is to prevent them from arising. A good shepherd should ever be on the alert to see possible danger signals and avoid letting them become problems. These signals may be seen in staff relations as well as in the membership of the church. Incidentally, this is another reason why you as the pastor should maintain a close relationship with both the staff and the people at large. In so doing you will be in a better position to deal with potential trouble spots before they become problems which erupt into conflagrations.

If the situation involves staff members, a conference with those involved may be all that is necessary. In the event it concerns a staff-member relationship, the obvious place to begin is with the staff member. Staff members should be a part of the solution, not of the problem. Should the condition continue a conference with the ones concerned together may be necessary. In case the member is at fault some trusted member such as a deacon might be asked to talk with that person. This may render a conference unnecessary. If possible it is better that the pastor not be involved personally. But when other measures fail, he should not hesitate to serve as a mediator. In such case it should be done in his role as pastor of the ones involved.

Then again a problem may be in the offing which involves you as the pastor himself. Faithfulness in your role as pastor will keep such to a minimum. But if for some reason "thy brother hath aught against thee" (Matt. 5:23), you should go to him and effect a reconciliation. The same is true if you have "aught" against a brother (Matt. 18:15). In each case you should take the initiative. This should be done in the spirit of Christ who took the initiative in effecting our reconciliation to God. Never will you stand taller as a pastor than when you do this.

It may be that you will inherit problems when you go to a new pastorate. In the event someone confronts you with such you should say kindly but firmly that you are not concerned about what took place before you accepted the pastorate, but that you are very much concerned about what will happen after that date. Even if you are not faced with them personally, it would be well to let word to that effect get around. I know from experience that it will wipe the slate clean so that you can start out afresh. You should not become involved in past problems of the church. In all likelihood there will be problems enough with which to deal in the future.

Every public figure can expect to receive anonymous letters. You should not be disturbed by them. A writer of such has a sick mind. My predecessor in a pastorate was disturbed by such. It was evident that they came from the same person. Shortly after going there I received three on successive days. From the typewriter markings I was certain that they were from the same person. When I told the chairman of deacons about them, he said "Oh, my! You will get disgusted and leave us!" I replied, "Oh, no! When I get such I am like a child at Christmas. I can hardly wait to open them to see what they say." He let this word get around. And I never received another from this person. Some anonymous letters will be vicious and some will not. Read them, file them in the wastebasket, and forget them.

If you endeavor to promote an active program you can expect to encounter problems. This is especially the case where innovation is involved. People are naturally fearful of new, untested things. And yet unless you lead your people to pioneer, they will lose interest in the old ways or else perform them mechanically. He was correct who said that the seven last words of a dying church are "We never did it that way before." New ideas and ways of doing things, therefore, should be devised. But they should be rooted in the basic purposes of the gospel. You, the staff, and the elected leadership should think through such carefully to be able to present them clearly to the congregation. It may be that a program has been tested elsewhere, but is new to your church. You should cite the experience of others so as to allay fears concerning new procedures.

But even then opposition may be forthcoming. Like old shoes, some people prefer the old and comfortable over the new and better. You should never ask your church to adopt a new program simply because you want it. It should be considered on its merits. If possible you should permit lay people to take the lead openly in order to avoid the above and also to prevent the danger of your confronting opposition personally. This is not an evidence of weakness but of strength in leadership. A good general does not lead the charge into battle. He plans, but leaves the execution of the plan to others. It will be well to present the matter to the deacons, who represent a cross section of church thinking, before bringing it before the church. If they reject it, you would be wise to drop it. If they recommend it to the church, its case will be strengthened thereby. While the congregation is the final authority, only in an extreme case would it be wise to take a matter to the church in defiance of the deacons.

In one instance, though I did not lead publicly in a controversial issue, my position was well known. So in the church business meeting when it was presented, I requested the chairman of deacons to serve as moderator. It was an accepted procedure by the people.

You should not flood the church with proposed new programs immediately upon assuming a new pastorate. You may find that the present program is better than yours. Even if this is not the case, you should first gain the confidence of the church in your leadership. I never proposed new departures from established procedures until I had been in a church at least six months. If the change is radical, a year would be better. The ideal time to inaugurate new programs is at the beginning of the church year. People are more likely to expect such then. But even then a blending of the good in the old with the new is preferable.

Where problems arise over procedure, not principle, there is one word, humanly speaking, which will provide a solution more than any other. W-A-I-T. We get in a hurry but God never does. If high pressure methods are necessary to get the church to adopt a program, you might well ask if it will succeed when adopted. Recently I was asked, "If your church voted on a program and it carried by a very small majority, what would you do?" The questioner agreed with me when I said that I would recommend that the church forego such a program. It is better to have a united church with a less efficient program than to have a better program and a divided church.

Problem Solving

From the above it is obvious that much of your time—too much, in fact—will be spent in either preventing or else in helping to solve problems. It is a time-consuming task, time which might be spent more profitably doing other things, if we lived in an ideal world. But since we do not, then that is a fact in a pastor's life. In a certain church the minister of education told a janitor to do something which was not a part of his routine duties. The janitor objected, "But I will get behind in my work." He was told that that was his work. Likewise, problem solving is a part of the pastor's work. It goes with the job. And since you want the job you must accep' his a' part of it. A lady objected to her butcher that he left too muc bone on the meat before weighing it. He replied in what would hardly classify as classic verse.

> You buy the field, you buy the stone;
> You buy the meat, you buy the bone.

Now in problem-solving you should begin with the problem-solver—yourself. This self-analysis has two purposes: to avoid becoming a problem yourself; and to understand yourself so that you can help others.

Since you spend so much time dealing with the problems of

individuals and groups, you should first spend time to evaluate yourself. Thus you should get in your study, close the door, and face yourself honestly with only God and you to hear and see. Instead of lying on a psychiatrist's couch, at least figuratively you should get on your knees before God. God himself should be your psychiatrist as he looks within your very soul and helps you to see yourself as he sees you. A psychiatrist cannot help a patient unless he receives honest answers to his questions. Neither can God help you unless you give honest answers to the questions he places in your mind. It is significant that God's first recorded question to Adam was "Where art thou?" (Gen. 3:9).

In order to start your mind to thinking in the proper direction let me pose some sample questions. Once you get into the matter you doubtless will ask many more.

Who am I? Whose am I? What kind of person am I? Am I patient, kind, loving, sympathetic, and understanding? Or am I impatient, fractious, cold, without feeling for others, selfish, and prejudiced? Am I weak or am I strong?

What kind of life do I live? Do I have skeletons in my closet? Do I live in a glass house? Can I take it when others point out my shortcomings? Or do I resent such? Do I hold a grudge against friends who in love remind me of my own failures? Or do I accept such in good grace and try to profit thereby?

Where am I? Why am I here? Who sent me here? Whom do I serve? And for what purpose? What is my role? A hired servant who works for wages? Or a shepherd who labors for the welfare of his sheep? Do I depend only upon my own strength? Or do I rely upon the power of God? Am I totally dedicated to Christ? What place do I give to the Holy Spirit in my ministry? Am I willing for God's will to be done absolutely in my life?

You should not answer these questions hurriedly, but only after sincere soul-searching. Where an honest answer calls for a negative response, you should make that an object of agonizing prayer. I suspect that this will be true of all of us.

Now having worked through the questions, I suggest that you

read Psalms 53, 31, and 23 in that order. Let the first be truly a confession of your own sins. In the second exult in the joy of forgiveness. In the third find the consolation that you are not alone in your ministry. Also let it remind you that as Jehovah is your shepherd you bear your role under the divine Shepherd. Once you have solved the problems in your own life you will be able better to help in solving those in the lives of others.

In dealing with the problems of others, whether it be those of persons or groups, you should identify with the persons involved. But you should endeavor not to become a part of the problems themselves. I remind you again that Jesus never took sides in a dispute. Rather he remained in the position which enabled him to speak to both sides. Except where morals or the basic truth of the gospel were concerned Paul did the same. In dealing with the problem of eating meat offered to idols (Rom. 14:1–21; 1 Cor. 8:1–13) he did identify with the strong faith (Rom. 14:14), but it was for the purpose of exhorting the strong to be considerate of the weak (Rom. 14:20–21; 1 Cor. 8:11–13). Once you do this for any other reason you become a part of the problem rather than a means for solving it. This does not mean that you should have no convictions, but rather that you should sublimate them for the greater goal of being a peacemaker.

In 1 Timothy 2:5 Paul spoke of Christ Jesus as the "mediator between God and man." The Greek text reads "one mediator of God and of man." Or that he partakes of the nature of both God and man. In that time a "mediator" was one appointed by the court to endeavor to resolve a problem between two people. He must impartially represent both parties and do all that was necessary to effect a reconciliation. It is in this light that we must understand Paul's usage. As deity Christ perfectly represented God. As humanity Jesus perfectly represented man. In his redemptive work he did all that was necessary to reconcile man to God. Thus when one believes in him as perfect Deity and perfect humanity, it is in Christ Jesus that God and man meet in reconciliation.

In a much lesser sense you are called upon to serve as a mediator between estranged parties. Without favoring one against the other you perfectly represent both. And you should do all in your ability by God's power to effect a reconciliation. The intended end is that, not in you but in your labor for the Lord, the estranged parties meet in reconciliation. In so doing you render a service to the people, but more vitally you are serving the Lord.

Unity in Diversity

These words should be the watchword for God's people everywhere. No two people are exactly alike—even those who have been recreated in Christ Jesus. Children of the same parents have certain resemblances, but they are also different. Even exact twins are different both in appearance and in temperament. Yet they comprise one family, and hopefully a harmonious one.

The same is true of God's children. They are alike but different. The only hope for harmony among them is that they permit their diversities to be overridden by a unity of purpose and effort for the Lord. Busy Christians are seldom problem Christians. Even a mule cannot kick and pull at the same time. As a child on a farm I recall how horses and mules became mean when we had a long wet spell during the season when we were tilling the soil. This was due to restless energy when all they did was eat, drink, and stay in the barn or barn lot. When they used up this energy by pulling a plow every day they were too tired at night to do anything but eat and rest. Christians are like that. To keep them peaceful they must be kept busy at a common task.

Somewhere I read about a man who owned a pack of valuable fox hounds. For a long time he had been too busy to take them hunting. So one day they got into a fight. The man saw his valuable property being chewed up by one another. He yelled, beat, and kicked them to no avail. When this failed he began to catch dogs by their legs and fling them as far as he could away from the fighting mass. But each one would get up and run right back into the pile. In desperation the man remembered that he had a fox in a pen. So he took it from the pen and loosed it where the dogs could see. Seeing the fox running away, like magic the dogs suddenly forgot their difference. As one they took off after the fox. Their diversity had found unity in a common interest and task.

So if you would have unity in diversity you must release a fox. Call it evangelism, missions, Bible study, visitation, steward- ship, or whatever. These are things in which Christians agree. Thus they become your foxes.

"A stitch in time saves nine." "Look before you leap." "An ounce of prevention is worth a pound of cure." Such proverbial sayings were not spun out of idle minds. They were refined in the hot crucible of experience. And you may well put them to use in your church program. The "stitch," "look," and "ounce" are efforts to keep your people busy. Thus they will not be inclined to major on minors. Busy people are happy people. So challenge your people with a gigantic task. Little nit-picking problems will vanish as mist before the morning sun. And as you march forth to meet the many challenges which are all about you, if you look back you will find yourself being followed by a happy, united people. Then you will not want to leave in an attempt to escape problems. You will pray that the Lord will leave you where you are—in a blessed and fruitful fellowship

Epilogue

Assuming that you have read thus far in this book, you are well aware of the fact that being a preacher/pastor is no easy task. When considered aright it is one of the most demanding of all vocations. You might think that I am trying to discourage you from becoming a preacher or continuing as one. To the contrary, I am endeavoring to encourage those who feel called of God to this work to accept the call and to offer counsel to young preachers with a view to helping them to become the best they are capable of being.

With design I have not asked you to look at the ministry through rose-colored glasses. One of the mistakes often made in enlisting workers in the church organizations is to play down the responsibilities involved. Many refuse because they feel that so easy a task is not worthy of their time. Others accept the position but have no concept of the duties involved. Thus they become ineffective workers. Many of these quit when the going gets rough.

The same may be said of many preachers. But if you know the difficulties and hard work involved, you are able to prepare yourself for them. The Lord needs all the harvest hands he can get. But he is looking for quality, not simply quantity. God reduced Gideon's band from thirty thousand to three hundred. But he knew that he could depend upon the smaller group, regardless of the hardships encountered. Jesus never courted the crowds. He always pointed to the responsibilities involved in following him. He is still looking for stouthearted men, not for those who simply go along for the ride.

Isaac Watts expressed this meaning in the words of "Am I a Soldier of the Cross." They apply to all Christians. But they should have a special meaning to us as preachers.

> Must I be carried to the skies
>   On flow'ry beds of ease,
> While others fought to win the prize
>   And sailed thro' bloody seas?

> Sure I must fight if I would reign;
>   Increase my courage, Lord!
> I'll bear the toil, endure the pain,
>   Supported by thy word.

When the apostle Paul wrote of the glory of the ministry, he emphasized the sufferings and responsibilities involved (2 Cor. 11:23–31). Speaking of his "thorn in the flesh," he told how he prayed that the Lord would remove it. But instead God promised him grace with which to bear it (2 Cor. 12:7–9). In response to the promise, he said, "Most gladly therefore will I rather glory in my infirmities [weaknesses], that the power of Christ may rest upon me. Therefore I take pleasure in infirmities, in reproaches, in necessities, in persecutions, in distresses for Christ's sake: for when I am weak, then I am strong" (2 Cor. 12:9–10). He was strong in weakness because he relied upon God whose strength is made perfect, or finds complete expression, in Paul's recognition of his weakness (v. 9).

Unworthy though we are, nothing more than brittle earthen vessels, we are the receptacles in which God has deposited his gospel and provided his grace and power. It is only in this spirit that we can measure up to the demands of our calling.

I would be wrong if I did not tell you that there are joys in the ministry. Because of the work we do and the people with whom we work, we should be the happiest people in the world. And the greatest happiness is to see some of the fruits of our labors in the souls and lives of men, women, boys, and girls. Notice that I said *some* of the fruits. Many of them you will never know until you arrive in glory.

But God is gracious as he permits us to see some of them on earth: souls won to Christ, Christians developing in and serving the Lord, families united in a mutual faith in Jesus—to name only a few. Also along the way we discover those long since forgotten but who remember us with undying gratitude. Paul referred to those to whom he had ministered "my joy and crown" (Phil. 4:1).

As I write these lines I have just returned from a Bible conference in the First Baptist Church, Maryville, Tennessee. One night a fine family in that church came up to remind me that I was their pastor at Dauphin Way in Mobile. The father said, "Thirty-two years ago you baptized me." Blessed words!

On the tenth anniversary of Harold Seever's pastorate at Dauphin Way as my successor, he invited me to preach. The evening before, he and Mrs. Seever took Mrs. Hobbs and me to dinner. As we were entering the eating place we met two couples coming out. Dr. Seever introduced us to them. In the conversation which followed one of the men said to me, "You won me to Christ." I expressed glad surprise and asked him when and where. He said, "It was while you were pastor of Calvary Baptist Church, Birmingham. One afternoon as a Junior boy I was on my way to attend the Royal Ambassador meeting. I met you in the hall, and you asked me if I were a Christian. When I told you I was not, you said, 'Come in here and sit down.' We went into a classroom where you won me to Christ. The following Sunday I made my profession of faith, and later you baptized me." He then told me that he had resigned a church in Mobile. The next morning he and his wife were leaving for Nashville, Tennessee, where he was to become the pastor of the Belmont Heights Baptist Church, one of the greatest churches in that city. His name is Bob Norman. Just a passing moment in the busy life of a pastor. But what a *moment!* Glory! Glory! Glory!

Yes, there is suffering and joy here and now. But the present joy is as nothing when compared with the joy of eternity. In Romans 8:16–18 Paul spoke to all believers. But for our purpose, again let me apply it to preachers.

"We are the children of God: And if children, then heirs; heirs of God, and joint-heirs with Christ; if so be that we suffer with him, that we may be also glorified together. For I reckon that the sufferings of this present time are not worthy to be compared with the glory which shall be revealed in us." In the Greek text Paul used three terms: heirs-with, sufferers-with, and glorified-with. All of these he related to Christ and to us.

The word rendered "reckon" is a bookkeeping term. So the apostle drew a balance in the books. "Worthy," you recall, connotes scales or balances. Paul placed the sufferings on one side of the scales and the glory on the other side. The eternal glory so far outweighs the sufferings that there is no comparison! We often say that God balances his books. No, he overbalances them—and in our favor!

Recently I gleaned from *The Parker Press* of the Parker Memorial Baptist Church, Anniston, Alabama, an excerpt from a sermon by John Bunyan entitled "The Heavenly Footman." It forms a fitting close to this little volume.

"1. Get into the way. 2. Then study on it. 3. Then strip, and lay aside everything that would hinder. 4. Beware of by-paths. 5. Do not gaze and stare too much about thee, but be sure to ponder the path of thy feet. 6. Do not stop for any that call after thee, whether it be the world, the flesh, or the devil; for all these will hinder thy journey, if possible. 7. Be not haunted with any discouragements thou meetest with as thou goest. 8. Take heed of stumbling at the cross. 9. Cry hard to God for an enlightened heart and a willing mind, and God give thee a prosperous journey."